To Tell a Story:
NARRATIVE
THEORY AND
PRACTICE

Papers Read at a
Clark Library Seminar
February 4, 1972

by Earl Miner, Paul Alpers,
Stanley E. Fish, and
Richard A. Lanham

With an Introduction by Robert M. Adams

William Andrews Clark Memorial Library
University of California, Los Angeles / 1973

Foreword

THE SEMINAR ON NARRATIVE that convened at the Clark Library on February 4th and 5th, 1972, was planned and organized by Professor Earl Miner of UCLA's Department of English, who was the Clark Library Professor for the 1971/72 academic year. Attendance at the meeting was limited to forty-five faculty members and graduate students from various University of California campuses. The sessions were moderated by Professor Robert M. Adams, also of the UCLA English Department, and under his guidance the discussion of the papers was lively and provocative.

The papers are published, with Professor Adams's introduction which puts them in context and summarizes their points of agreement and disagreement, to serve as a permanent record for the participants, and to stimulate discussion among that wider audience to which they now are addressed.

WILLIAM E. CONWAY
Librarian,
William Andrews Clark
Memorial Library

Introduction

Robert M. Adams

D ESCRIBING AN EVENT—that is, telling a story—is so simple and natural a process, so primitive and idle an activity, it involves such an effortless blossoming of language, that we shall never come to the end of analyzing it. A single simple parable can act as a prism, refracting a full spectrum of whatever critical light we put into it. The conference on seventeenth-century narrative, held at the Clark Library of UCLA on February 4th and 5th, 1972, might have seemed condemned to deal with a sparse subject matter. By comparison with the eighteenth and nineteenth centuries, the seventeenth is not rich in achieved narrative performance. There is indeed that supreme epic just two-thirds of the way through the century; but then ... We have some scattered gropings at the novel; we have one or two major histories; and we have narrative poems in some profusion, but with strong and sometimes overwhelming didactic overtones. The greater riches lie nearby in the realms of drama: yet the drama betrays anti-narrative bias by a leaning toward masque at the beginning of the century and a penchant for opera and operatic effects at the end. Elsewhere, the lesser forms chosen by the century—the anatomy, the character, the diary, the informal essay, the sermon, the polemical pamphlet—almost all seem designed to frustrate narrative expectations as much as to satisfy them.

And yet, as the Clark conference unfolded, it became apparent that simply to touch the topic of narrative at any stage in its development was to enter upon some of the central critical problems of modern language-theory. Without any preconcerted plan, the panelists divided sharply along the axis of mimetic versus structured use of language—that is, according to the degree of autonomous, and by implication antithetical, structure they were willing to envisage in a basically mimetic and linear pattern of narrative. Indeed, the relatively contaminated quality of seventeenth-century narrative served neatly to complement the suspicious and disintegrative eye of the critics. Those of them who chose to step outside the sequential and linear patterns of seventeenth-century narrative, as very recent trends have encouraged them to do, found a great many interesting things going on there, a great many ratios of complement and counteraction to be calculated.

Schematizing and oversimplifying as one must in order to set up a pattern of broad relationships, we found Professor Miner proposing the most conservative and Aristotelian view of narration, most inclined to accept the thesis that poetic "middles" should develop in a linear way to connect beginnings with ends sequentially in order to produce unified and harmonious effects upon readers. That this is a frequent, a normative pattern even, there cannot be much doubt. But what happens when middles refuse this their normal function (thereby casting doubts on beginnings and ends)—what happens when a list or a rhetorical display or a different sort of logic imposes itself on the sequence of events, deliberately damming or distracting it from its self-appointed end? Do we attach that norm—doubtful as it is—to a set of value judgments? Evidently middles are not bound to take the shortest track between two points; how far can a middle wander, how wide a gap can it ask us to jump, before it ceases to be an achieved middle? And if it does so cease, what then? These were some of the topics raised by the paper and canvassed by the audience.

Professor Alpers, in his discussion of narrative "mode," called attention to this curiously undefined and useful word, representing it as a measure of the relation between reader or writer and the world of the literary work. So redefined, mode is not simply part of a self-sufficient literary structure, but a bond of understanding by which a narrative manipulates its readers in a whole complex of non-narrative dimensions. By widening the range of ways in which a narrative can relate to its readers, Mr. Alpers thus spoke for a more psychological and less formal understanding of the way in which narratives are articulated. Indeed, the questioning that followed dwelt on the question whether the range of alternatives made available for judgment was not too wide to allow of any precise formulations. The "mode" of a narrative as Mr. Alpers defined it anew was obviously useful and realistic in supplementing Mr. Miner's model of the pattern by which a narrative works on a reader; but didn't it let almost too many cats out of the bag at once? It saved mimesis from a formula, but at what cost?

Professor Fish, without casting mimesis aside altogether, undertook to show that in the highly patterned prose of Lancelot Andrewes the sequential nature of Aristotelian narrative may be set aside, and a sentence convey its meaning by the violent adjustments of expectation, attitude, and definition that it forces on the reader, long before it works out its full syntax. Because it seeks to evoke a special kind of inward, timeless, and universal vision, Christian narration may thus develop a kind of cross-narrative or anti-narrative dimension, which enables the answer to find the questioner even in the process of articulating the question. Thus middle becomes end, or end middle. Of course there was an immediate outcry for definitions. Didn't Mr. Fish's theory apply better to Euphuistic prose, for example, than to Christian prose like that of Bunyan? No, Mr. Fish did not think so; he made bold to question the true linearity of Bunyan's book, effectually depriving the Pilgrim of his Progress, and reaffirmed (with aid and comfort from Roland Barthes) the special atemporal counter- or cross-narrative quality of Christian discovery.

In the last paper of the day, Professor Lanham audaciously undertook to rehabilitate the *logoi,* the set speeches, both of historical writers and of sophists and rhetoricians. He conceded them to be interruptions of historical narrative, and hostile in their formal patterning to all sorts of mimetic values, but saw in their patterned formulae elements of authenticity with regard to experience and of structural validity independent of experience, which entitled them at least to a dialectical parity with the truths of mimetic speech, even in the purified form appropriate to philosophy. Here again discriminations seemed called for: it seemed one thing for rhetoric to be meaningful because it exposed the fallacies of rhetoric, another for it to have value in and of itself. Mr. Lanham was challenged, and he replied vigorously.

In thus roughly, all too roughly, summarizing these four papers, whose merits require no eulogy from me, I intend only to show how closely their arguments dovetailed, or even joined. Mr. Fish directly confronted the approach of Mr. Miner; Mr. Lanham's dialectic of rhetoric and philosophy could hardly avoid defining a "mode" in the sense used by Mr. Alpers. Seventeenth-century narrative, for all its sparsity and perhaps because it was trying to handle more relationships that it could always control securely, was revealed to have unsuspected richness and to pose for the modern analyst problems of unanticipated complexity.

What in effect we see here is a nice instance of the process by which new critical perceptions, however remote the areas giving rise to them, are drawn into the texture of literary discussions and revaluations with long and complex histories of their own.

That M. Roland Barthes should inspire a fresh look at the prose style of Lancelot Andrewes seems to me in the highest degree exhilarating. That rhetorical tropes which have been denigrated for years as artificial and insincere should now be defended on the grounds that they are artificial and insincere is almost equally exhilarating. What we press towards, from varying directions, is a perception of the many different relations in which language can stand to its "subject"—and of the extent to which that subject includes interference from language itself. Though phrased as a limitation on language, this condition may evidently be turned to direct advantage; the seventeenth century, compelled to cope with multiplying points of view and light from many different sources, practiced an agility in its narrations which we are perhaps only now in a position to appreciate. The difficulty looming on the horizon—incorporate, for the moment, in the sinister figure of M. Paul deMan—is that we shall be forced to examine our own critical dialects as varieties of literary language which, if they don't actually compel us to see and say certain things and don't peremptorily forbid us to see and say certain others, at least exert strong controlling influences. Before examining a text, we shall have to analyze the language in which we propose to analyze it—using, for the purpose, language which, etc. What is sometimes called, a bit portentously, "metacriticism" will thus have disintegrated its way back to "precriticism," an activity capable of indefinite prolongation, and not really of much interest until applied to a text, from which its inherent logic is to recede with all deliberate haste.

These enchanting developments may, indeed, lie in the future. For the present, the conversations at the Clark not only focussed, for the most part, on specific texts; they offered, as it seemed to me, a liberating sense of the various fresh ways in which seventeenth-century narrations can be understood to work on us, even after so many readings and so many years. As an ob-

ix

server whose loyalties are divided (sometimes torn) between at least two fields (the seventeenth century and the twentieth), I sense a most fruitful collaboration at work here. It seems to me, for instance, that a great many of the rhetorical issues agitated by Mr. Lanham have roots that he himself could easily trace back through Burke to an exercise like the "Oxen of the Sun" episode of *Ulysses*. I suspect Mr. Alpers' concern with widening the definition of "mode" has been heightened by the practice of Yeats and Eliot in invoking through their poetry the active complicity of the reader. As for Mr. Fish, I can hardly think that, in discussing the art of Lancelot Andrewes, he didn't have somewhere tantalizingly in his mind the counter-pointed rhythm of a pair of sentences like:

Grossbooted draymen rolled barrels dullthudding out of Prince's stores and bumped them up on the brewery float. On the brewery float bumped dullthudding barrels rolled by grossbooted draymen out of Prince's stores. (*Ulysses*, "Aeolus")

Finally, Mr. Miner, in effectively accepting an anti-middle as a true middle, bore witness to the domestication of *Waiting for Godot* in our literary value-structure.

In a word, all of our critics were and are men deeply rooted in the present tense; that they find so many new qualities in (and approaches to) the literature of the remote past is almost a measure of their sensitivity to the currents of the present. But I shan't insist on this topic, as what T. S. Eliot said about poets (in "Tradition and the Individual Talent") obviously applies to critics with equal force and in both directions.

The paradoxical endeavor of the critic, to say something newer and newer about a work of art that is constantly getting older and older, is not, after all, self-defeating, but self-renew-ing. As in an Ibsen play, we advance a short step toward the future only by way of an immense retrogression into our un-organized past—re-enacting, thereby, the archetypal destiny of

x

another dramatic hero, M. Jourdain, who was also delighted to have a fine name for what he had been doing all along. For, after all, describing an event, which is simply telling a story, was a simple and natural process, performed with consummate skill and tact by myriad-minded narrators, long before they had critics and scholars to explain to other scholars and critics just what they had been about. To paraphrase a high authority, the secret working of the literary process may be found, in part, of them that seek it; but of them that sought it not never but found.

I

Distributing the Middle: Problems of "Movement" in Narrative Poetry

EARL MINER

L<small>ET US IMAGINE</small> that on a certain day in 1651 John Milton opened a book labeled *Gondibert* and started to read: "Of all the *Lombards,* by their Trophies knowne . . ." And that a day or so later Milton concluded: "For give it any air the flames will rage." We have rudely imagined the beginning and ending of a literary experience of a poem which its author declared was but half complete and which was never to be completed. Now let us imagine that one of us is reading *Paradise Lost* again. He sits down, opens the book, and begins: "Of Mans First Disobedience . . ." Some time later he reaches the last line: "Through *Eden* took their solitarie way." Two beginnings, two endings. And two very different experiences of the vast middles between. Milton reading Davenant and we reading Milton obviously constitute two quite different experiences. Milton read a large fragment, we read a complete poem. In one instance a seventeenth-century reader has read a work by a contemporary poet, in the other one of us has read a work published something over three hundred years ago. Among the problems involved are some that claim special attention. What constitutes that great middle between beginning and ending? What ought that to be? What is it? What necessary constituents does it have?

None of these questions can find anything like full answer

here, but they are of sufficient importance to have been worth even Aristotle's notice that a tragedy should follow the order of beginning, middle, and ending. His remark has been more often repeated than amplified. It is true that, some five or so centuries after the Stagirite, Dionysius or Longinus remarked on the sublimity of that passage in the scriptures of the Jews in which God says, " 'Let there be light,' and there was light."[1] Years later, in 1967, Frank Kermode published *The Sense of an Ending*. And in 1970 there appeared Philip Stevick's study, *The Chapter in Fiction: Theories of Narrative Division*. It is true that others have touched on the Aristotelian topics, especially the classicists, and, what is nearly the same thing, the Germans. It does not seem, however, that my subject has obsessed mankind. My remarks on the middle of the literary parenthesis would seem to give me title for inclusion not so much among the Peripatetics as the Somnambulists.

"And how shall I begin?" Deferring once again to critical commonplaces, I shall take my beginning *in medias res,* in the middle of Dr. Johnson's life of Milton. *Paradise Lost* "has," he wrote, "distinctly and clearly what Aristotle requires, a beginning, a middle, and an end."[2] The "intermediate parts" of *Samson Agonistes,* however, "have neither cause nor consequence, neither hasten nor retard the catastrophe."[3] Johnson demanded "regular and consequential distribution"[4] of the middle, believing an irregular and undistributed middle as illogical as did the strictest schoolman examining a syllogism.

Since in this matter Aristotle, like Aeneas in another, was *primus ab oris,* we may linger a few moments on the implications of passages in the *Poetics,* especially as they have been recently glossed for us by Gerald F. Else.[5] In his seventh chapter Aristotle defines a "middle" as "that which both follows another thing and has something else following it." It has not been sufficiently appreciated that he meant "middle" plurastically, as *each* of the several episodes between the beginning and

4

the ending.⁶ That large middle, consists, then, of many middles, and what is true of tragedy must *a fortiori* be truer yet of narrative poems, not least (one must add) of most seventeenth-century poetic narratives. The same seventh chapter makes clear that Aristotle held that the events or middle parts of a work should take so consequential an order that removal or repositioning would cause confusion or misshapenness. Shapeliness stands as an Aristotelian ideal, because his metaphors for literature are the common ones of "animate bodies and constructed objects."⁷

Surely it is no disservice to the state of criticism to suggest that metaphors for literature should not be taken as definitions, and my urging is the sincerer because I think Aristotle's images, common though they be, are misleading. It may be worth a reminder that Aristotle's view of ethics held almost exclusively that actions rather than states and attitudes constitute moral determinants, because in this we—in our more subjective, psychological approach to human behavior—often find ourselves separated from him by more than twenty-three centuries alone. Yet our Greek master hints at one important distinction between the plots of plays and epics. In his twenty-fourth chapter he remarks on the dramatist's subjection to the forward movement of time. Any stoppage to recall the past endangers our sense of dramatic movement. The narrative poet exercises greater freedom, and some few do indeed have a beginning *in medias res,* so as to require lengthy recapitulation. Only after the third book of the *Aeneid* has Virgil recapitulated the past, and later Anchises, Helenus, and others interrupt, without strain, the forward movement to dwell on past or future events.

In other words, the narrated middle, or middles, as opposed to the dramatized middle of traditional theatre, uses great freedom in handling a narrated time scheme. The narrated time need not follow the actual chronology of events, much less proportion the time required for narration to the temporal

5

proportion of the events themselves. In *Paradise Lost,* Raphael's story of the war in heaven recapitulates a three-days battle, although Milton presents that story as taking less than a day to tell, and although only an hour or so is required to read it. As Günther Müller observed in his German way, narrative time involves both "Erzählzeit und erzählte Zeit," the time of narrating process and the time-span narrated.[8] The dominion over our sense of time possessed by narrative poets sometimes approaches the despotic.

The narrative middle can be regarded metaphorically as an articulated living thing or as a structured object. Not only can it be, but it usually is. The metaphor misleads, however, by substituting an image for Müller's dual temporal process which is, with our memory, the sole thing that we readers know from experience as poems. If we speak without metaphor of our experience of a poem, it is perfectly obvious that one aspect of the dual reading process is our present consciousness proceeding from the beginning to the end. Human consciousness experiences only one order of the present, its own. But since that presence of consciousness possesses duration in time, and since the mind also includes memory and anticipation, the present consciousness proceeds in time, creating from the coded symbols of the text a literary experience that increasingly accumulates in the memory as an aesthetic past and an increasingly diminishing, clarifying aesthetic future in the anticipation.

Very simply, when we talk about literature or a given narrative, what we actually speak of does not constitute an object with a structure, but rather an experience like any other: with the one exception that we regard it as aesthetic, provisional, and derived from words. More accurately, when we talk about literature, we speak of *remembered* experience. One experience of reading is distinguished from another by the reader—depending on which reader or which given reader at a given time—and

6

by the text to which he brings to bear what alone he has, himself.

Like the poet's distribution of the narrative middle, the reader's has a further temporal element common to literary experience of many kinds. The mind engages with the actual order of occurrences in the poem in that order of occurrence, no matter how unchronological, and it engages with what it sorts out as the presumed order of "historical" chronology. The engagement itself constitutes that temporal experience in which, after we begin to read, we accumulate a remembered past sequence of what we have read and an anticipated future sequence. Each reading possesses its own history or, in more fashionable language, its own phenomenology. What each of us remembers and expects possesses a significance derived from the discreteness of what is observed: as an aesthetic experience, it is discrete from nonaesthetic experience but similar; and as an experience with its own history, it is discrete from the actual order of occurrence, from imagined historical chronology, and from other readings of the same poem by the same reader. To lose sight of such differences means that we confuse the aesthetic or provisional nature of art in *Absalom and Achitophel* with Restoration and biblical history; or that we believe literary experience unique in being repeatable, outside of time.

Such considerations bring us to one of the most obvious and most difficult problems of all in narrative: sequence. What is narrative sequence? How does it differ from nonnarrative literary sequences? Although sequence provides the basis of narrative, it proves very difficult to define a narrative sequence without resorting to synonyms or tautologies. Our difficulties are not lessened by the presence of the temporal orders I have been discussing. A narrative obviously has a sequence in the poet's creation and in our recreation. Surely a central feature of that sequence derives from our simple sense that of two events not occurring simultaneously one must precede the other.

7

With Aristotle, we expect or demand that the succession of events has a logic, but those of us skeptically inclined may wonder if in long narrative works certain things could not be reordered without damage. Must Homer's catalogue of the ships come just where it does? Have not countless people read James's novel *The Ambassadors* without noticing that two chapters were out of their order? All I am arguing is that sequence in itself may give pleasure, as in *The Arabian Nights* or the *Decameron*. More than that, a certain randomness may also give pleasure—as Butler, Swift, and Sterne so capitally discovered for us. Yet when all is said by way of exception, we anticipate from the sequence of literary experience some *informative* logic.

I use the word "informative" with emphasis for a double reason. For one thing, that logic of the well distributed middle constitutes nothing other than the complex *form* assuming in our minds. And for another, that logic ensures that the sequence *informs* us, becoming intelligible, significant, meaningful. To say it another way, we expect in reading that what we move through in sequence will possess significance *in* that sequence, by virtue of a meaningful movement. Seventeenth-century English poetic narrative illustrates with many brave attempts and some glorious failures how difficult significant movement is to create. In 1642 there appeared Sir Francis Kynaston's *Leoline and Sydanis* and Henry More's ΨΥΧΩΔΙΑ *Platonica: or a Platonical Song of the Soul*. Kynaston created a lovely, witty movement with no special significance whatever. More's poem turns out to be a high-minded, fierce, neo-Platonic allegory exasperating in style and pointless in its movement. At one point, Ahad, who marries his daughter Psyche to his son Aeon, proceeds to marry them both himself, and the three climb into bed. As Horace well said, when we are given such nonsense, disbelief renders odious, and it helps not a whit that Ahad, Aeon, and Psyche constitute a neo-Platonic trinity analogous to the Christian. One does not catch Plato himself in such absurdity. Other problems

8

appear within a decade. Davenant's *Gondibert* simply stops about half-way done, and Cowley's *Davideis* one-third. There can be no more radical deficiency in significant movement than the impossibility of completing the movement.

I do not mean to belittle either poem, but the absolute problems of both are mirrored in what we have of them. Davenant employs a typical narrative dodge as old as Thucydides: the stop-and-go technique of giving now movement in narration, now significance in set speeches. He gives us rattling action here and significant interruption there. In little, the interruptive significances lie like sententious acorns in the forest of the active hunt. In large, the interruptive significances may run for as long as the two fascinating cantos telling of the house and temple of the sage Astragon.⁹ To compare great things to small, it was precisely by refusing in anger to let movement and significance join, only by arguing that reason and action show the world to be irrational and in the stocks, that Butler made stop-and-go into that terrible great poem, *Hudibras*. Milton himself ran grave risks at two points in *Paradise Lost:* with the speeches in Heaven and with the audio-visual historical lecture by Michael. Highly significant these episodes may be, but they strain our sense of informative sequence, of occurrent reality. Dryden also seeks saving tricks in *Absalom and Achitophel* by using surrogates for narrative movement; and Old Testament semi-narrative is called upon to make it seem that the semi-narrative of events in his own day actually moves.

Plainly, the logic of narrative movement involves many features, not all of which are necessary for literary greatness in any instance. Among the matters that I must omit, two principal ones haunt me: the historicity, the seventeenth-centuryness of the poems, and also the conditions making a fit reader. What I can stress is that the informative logic of the middle involves not merely sequence but also consequence. We can charge a sequence with *non sequitur* and mean that it does not make

9

sense. The sequence itself must be intelligible, signifying, and therefore meaningful and moving. So must also be the constituents of that sequence: characters, events, places, times, relationships, social and moral orders, and so on. But we must find something more if we are to deliver ourselves to the poet. As our consciousness proceeds in reading, in accumulating a remembered past and an anticipated future, our sense of significant sequence must include *con*sequences.

By stressing *con*sequences I imply a logic, not merely sequence. I also imply those things not in the sequence as sequence but *with* it by virtue of recognizable rhythms, iterations, parallels, echoes, and the like. Much in fact of what proves most satisfyingly significant are the consequences revealed by sequence. *Paradise Lost* would seem a poorer poem without its emphasis throughout on the threat of darkness and the promise of light, without the imagery of flora or desolation, of holding hands and separation, of parenthood and childhood, with many other *con*sequences emerging from sequence. Yet another important consequence, in my usage of the term, is provided by answerable style. Strictly speaking, style provides elements of syntactic and imagistic sequence, but although we experience it temporally as we do all else, it assists in giving us that seemingly atemporal Miltonness of Milton or Drydenness of Dryden. Style only assists; for although all of us would have difficulty imagining *Paradise Lost* or *Absalom and Achitophel* apart from their distinctive language, prosody, and syntax, in fact they have been rendered into Latin, French, Japanese, and other languages in which they appear perforce in alien garb but with something of their essence remaining. Another poem, William Chamberlayne's extraordinary and unjustly neglected *Pharonnida* will occupy me a bit later. For it, style is one of the chief consequences of the poem and I doubt that translation could possibly leave it a significant work.

We cannot ignore another feature of the movement or

middles of narrative poems, the role played by conventions or more especially, perhaps, by conventional ideas about those conventions. I shall begin with a fiction held by some seventeenth-century narrative poets, that their stories were ordered on the five-act structure of plays. Davenant argues the case best for *Gondibert*.[10] But it will not do. Significantly, in his other "Lombard" work, the tragedy of *Albovine,* he allows himself no equivalent of his two-canto digression on Astragon. We simply have no sense of a play in his narrative. Chamberlayne completed his design in *Pharonnida* with five books of five cantos each, but the poem resembles a *Bildungsroman* more than a play. It seems that, by distorting Aristotle, men like Davenant and Hobbes convinced themselves that the only difference between tragedy and epic lay in the mode of presentation.[11] They went too far in what was surely an important critical truth. For if God the Father does speak like a school divine in *Paradist Lost,* the point is that He, the Son, and many of the angels could not credibly be represented speaking at all in a play. The five-act construction turns out to have been critical phlogiston.

Some of our assumptions also arouse doubt. For instance, we assume that it is a major convention of the epic that the story have a beginning *in medias res,* and in such a way as to require subsequent long relation or retrospection of events. Without doubt, retrospection is a major element of narrative.[12] Certainly the idea that the beginning *in medias res* should require a lengthy relation of matters skipped over is highly pertinent to *Paradise Lost.* That poem is, however, the sole seventeenth-century English poem I know of that so begins. The *Aeneid* also begins that way. But the following classical poems do not, much as they manipulate time in other ways: the *Iliad* and the *Odyssey;* the *Pharsalia;* the *Thebiad* and *Achilleid* of Statius; the *Punica* of Silius Italicus and the *Mosella* of Ausonius; as well as the *Apotheosis, Hamartigenia,* and *Psychomachia* of Prudentius.[13] The evidence requires that we set the *Aeneid* and

Paradise Lost apart. We discover in Virgil that he adjusts to chronology by the end of Book III, or after one quarter of the poem. In *Paradise Lost* Milton exceptionally withholds that adjustment until the end of Book VIII, or two-thirds of the poem. The spring Milton coils so tightly in us as we read, to give us such powerful release in Books IX and X, is no epic commonplace: it is a Virgilian device taken to lengths that only Milton could have done.

We believe that another major feature of narrative movement is the provision of a moment when the informative sequence takes its most decisive turn. That peripeteia or climax perhaps comes at the slaying of Hector in the *Iliad* and the slaying of the suitors in the *Odyssey,* but I would not stake my money on either one. And what of the *Aeneid?* As the enormous popularity of the first two books of *Paradise Lost* shows, something more than the Aristotelian *mythos* is involved. With Virgil it is unquestionably the case that for centuries the Dido episode of Book IV and the descent to the underworld in Book VI have seemed most important. But as Dryden additionally observed, Virgil modeled the former half of the *Aeneid* on the *Odyssey* and the latter on the *Iliad.*[14] The slaying of Turnus provides but a last and not necessarily the most affecting climax in our reading. I share the belief that the most important climax of *Paradise Lost* comes to us three-quarters of the way through the poem, whatever the numerological symbolists may wish to say about the mystical center, or the Romantics about Satan. On the other hand, *Paradise Regained* and *Absalom and Achitophel* carefully employ a series of what may best be thought anticlimaxes until the sudden reversal on the last page.

Such simple matters, such important matters, seem to me good evidence to prove that we must seek to remember our actual experience of reading more attentively than the admittedly useful commonplaces that tell of literary possibilities. We need to urge ourselves and our students to thaw into renewed life poets like Milton, Dryden, and Butler that we have frozen into inaction by calling them classics. Of course they are classics, but so are Dickens and Joyce, Proust and Mann, not to mention some among our contemporaries. By the same token, Milton, Dryden, and Butler remain radically new, avant-garde, experimental, innovative, and all those other attributes so readily assigned to that most transient of states, the modern. Whether so-called "classic" or "modern," the important narratives share alike in that height of quality that is positive about a "classic," and in that radical reorganization of experience that literature requires in order to seem forever new and exciting. Chaucer and Spenser, Pope and Wordsworth, with yet others deserve the same recognition of that radically meaningful narrative movement for which originality remains the simplest term.

The sense of climax in our experience of the poem turns out to be as crucial for Butler's *Hudibras* as for almost any other English narrative, although Butler, who is garbed in rue, certainly wears it with a difference. The narrative point of *Hudibras* is bludgeoned into us tirelessly: human creatures so misuse their reason that any sort of meaningful action is delayed seemingly endlessly by fruitless harangue. And when a climax becomes at last inevitable, it comes to us as hideous anticlimax. If we allow ourselves Aristotle's metaphor of *architectonikē,* we can say that Butler erects in our angry hearts a Tower of Babel consisting for the most part of random scaffolding and constant danger of falling wood and stone. That, it must be said again, is his point. He wishes to arouse in us the same sense that he feels of maddening irrelevance, of ceaseless frustration, and all but unremitting pain. That great scabby poem does indeed scratch where it itches—*ubi dolor ubi digitus,* as Burton said— and Butler's nails always go where it hurts most. His climax occurs never and ever, and he makes his anguish, his anger our own.

13

Seventeenth-century narrative concludes with Dryden's *Fables Ancient and Modern,* completed late in 1699 and published in 1700. In this wonderfully mellow collection, Dryden somehow managed to wrest from disease and old age a health and youth that it had seemed the principal business of narrative poetry earlier in the century to deny. Like Milton and Dryden, I shall not exercise modesty unduly; I shall say that my interpretation of the *Fables* as a work that integrates a number of individual poems seems to have been accepted. That being the case, I shall assume the integration, and observe that in reading the *Fables* from beginning to end the sense of climax in the individual stories is very marked. Apart from all else, the preponderance of selections from the *Metamorphoses* assists in giving us an experience of numerous episodes rising to crisis and achieving resolution. Making a whole of disparate parts may be thought a version of that grand commonplace of the century, *concordia discors.* But a reader today beginning with that beautifully mythopoeic poem to the Duchess of Ormonde and ending with *Cymon* and *Iphigenia,* rendered poetry from the prose of Boccaccio, has the strong sense that he has experienced a sequence of images of human lives that combines to create in his mind and heart a generous image of humanity. Struggling for the most part in vain to achieve the good life, we engage in numerous actions of tentative meaning and assurance. We try, we fail, or we seem to succeed. The repetition drives home the problem of cognition—how do we know the world and ourselves? In the end, human life seems wonderfully precious and at the same time to derive ultimate meaning only from the ultimate source: God.

Butler, Dryden, and Milton appeared as narrative poets in that order, although their relative status must seem the reverse to us all. But what of the other narrative poets between 1640 and 1700? A study of the "Secular Heroic Epic Poetry of the Caroline Period" decides that Chalkhill's *Thealma and Clear-*

chus, as also Chamberlayne's *Pharonnida,* combine "elements
of the Spanish romances, of the pastoral and its offspring, the
historical allegory" with yet more "of the matter and method
of the Greek romances," ennobling them to epic status.[15] Saints-
bury was more succinct: he had to read *Pharonnida* three times
merely to write his résumé. Such was the teeming sense of life
in a tumultuous England, and so poets sought to find in poetry
what they could not in life. *Paradise Lost* vindicates what Milton
could not find in the 1640's and 1650's, and Dryden's *Fables*
reviews life after three revolutions in the state. And where is
the middle of my own narrative? I think that I would choose
1659 when *Pharonnida* appeared. Although the poem is not as
well known as it deserves to be, it certainly provides me an end
in medias res with a vengeance, and with the suggestion that
there is more to narrative theory and to seventeenth-century
poetic practice than has been said. In Book III, canto iii, the
Turkish woman Janusa tries adulterously and vainly to seduce
the hero, Argalia. In this piquant situation, Chamberlayne
writes,

> In this, as hot and fierce a Charge of Vice,
> As (since he lost the field in Paradice)
> Man ever felt; the brave *Argalia* sits,
> With Vertue coold in Passions feaverish Fits:
> Yet at Lifes Garrisons his Pulses beat,
> In hot Alarums, till to a soft Retreat
> Cal'd by that fair Commandress spight of all
> Beauties prevailing Rhetorick, though he fall,
> Ruin'd beneath her anger, he by this
> Unwelcome Language, her expected bliss,
> Converts to rage ... (III, iii, 471–81)

And so on, for another eleven and a half lines rejecting Janusa,
before that sentence, the period, and the verse paragraph end.
The canto, and my middle, end as she leaves the room:

> the Room she leaves
> To her Contemner, who not long receives

15

The benefit of rest, she that had been
The Prologue unto this obstructed sin,
With six arm'd Slaves was enterd, thence to force
Him to his dismal Jayl, but the Divorce
Of life, from those which first approacht, joynd to
The others flight had put her to renew
That scattered strength, had not that sacred tye
(His solemn Oath) from Laureld Victory,
Snatcht the fair wreath, and though brave Valour strives
To reach at Freedome through a thousand Lives:
At her Command more tamely made him yield,
Then conquerd Virgins in the Bridal Field.   (511–24)

So poets and we readers traverse what Sidney called the zodiac of wit, and so the best narratives begin and end, finding ways to make of many middles a significant narrative movement, taking us along with those old men from the chimney corner, and children from their games.

Postscript

SINCE PROFESSOR ADAMS had seen our papers in advance, he had prepared some questions for each of us that started a very lively discussion. In addition to the volley of remarks, there must have been other questions left unvoiced and which the reader of this printed version may also wish to raise. The questions Professor Adams addressed to me were prefaced by mention of certain problematic works such as *Tristram Shandy,* that great favorite of all our discussions about prose narrative. He has in effect repeated some of his questions in the Introduction and so I may repeat something of my replies. He asked what one is to make of the "middles" of two seventeenth-century poems, Crashaw's lugubrious celebration of the Magdalene, *The Weeper,* and Dryden's celebration of discrete events of 1666 in *Annus Mirabilis.* My reply was that we brought to such poems criteria of interest and coherence such as we apply to events in life. Crashaw uses a simple, an over-simple, principle of order, a kind of clothes-line of damp washing arranged as to table linen, towels, clothes, and so forth. We recognize the lines of order but do not find them particularly engaging. Events in 1971 provide an analogy for events in 1666. An account of the Indochinese war, of the American rapprochement to the People's Republic of China, and of the disturbances in Ireland could find some degree of relation between the first two but would strain mightily to find a connection between the second and the third. *Annus Mirabilis* succeeds in part in relating the Second Dutch War to the Great Fire of London, but it shows strains in making the relation.

One of the most enlightening questions from the floor concerned our ability to distinguish the end of the beginning and the beginning of the end: in other words the limits of the "middles." Obviously, after our sense of beginning we have begun, and we have no sense of ending before we do so. But I take it that the questioner really inquired about what lies between, and that is more difficult. Our reading shows such a between to involve a continuum in which Aristotle's pluralistic middles are articulated. The sense of continuing makes it extremely difficult to define what we yet know to exist, those constituent elements of narrative that we term episodes, scenes, and speeches. But then, at last notice, linguists were unable to define "syllable" any better. In the process of our literary experience, we recognize that the elements constituting the literary continuum are cognitively different, but that the differences involve an intelligible development of certain common elements—characters, a voyage, etc. Such a conception of literary movement is referred to in my paper in terms of the "informative" character of literary experience. If we think of the movement as something more than the hum of continuing or the babel of discreet chatter— if we think of it as having an informative or intelligible development—then I think we are within grasp of understanding how what "moves" also "means."[16]

A wholly different set of problems was raised by some questions concerning the issue of randomness vs. order in narrative movement. On this matter I feel that both my remarks and the problem were not fully understood. I say in the paper that the narrator may deploy the "middles" with great freedom and that randomness may give pleasure. But I held and I still hold that however free or random a work may seem to be, it must achieve a degree of intelligibility; it must be "informative." My stand derives from the nature of the mind's operations. Perception and cognition (along with many affective forms of understanding) demand as it were a syntax rather than mere sound. A wide latitude of freedom can be enjoyed, but total anarchy makes no sense. Randomness may give pleasure, but a totally random sorting by a computer of the words in *Paradise Lost* would not prove intelligible. I argued that Herrick's "sweet disorder" came near the point, and that the limits of randomness could also suggest the limits of order. My position was challenged by the example of *Finnegans Wake*. As I tried to stress in my paper, I do not believe that something termed either classical or experimental holds any privileged status. Either Joyce satisfies minimal claims to signification or the sound and fury signify nothing. As a *reductio ad absurdum,* I proposed the reading of *Finnegans Wake* backwards which, like the playing backwards of a tape of Bach's St. Matthew Passion, is gibberish. On that head I am well content to be thought conservative and Aristotelian.

My paper derives in considerable measure from two studies on which I have been engaged. One is a theoretical study of the nature of literary experience that postulates (contra Aristotle) that a "poem" exists not as an object but as a transformation by the reader of the coded symbols of a text. This transformation (I argue) employs all that is in the reader as that all is brought to bear. A literary "work" represents the transformation by a "poet" of all that is in him as his all is brought to bear in the act of transformation. The difference between a poet's and a reader's transformations can be represented by saying that each transformation by the poet (as poet and not as a reader) produces another work, a *Macbeth* after a *Hamlet,* whereas the reader's transformations produce so many *Hamlets* or *Macbeths.* There is no present need to enter into all that is involved, but the mention of such matters may clarify certain aspects of my paper and, in particular, my unsympathetic response to Aristotle's mimetic-affective theory. The other study is a so-to-speak "new literary history" of seventeenth-century English poetry, the third in a series of three. The first two (*The Metaphysical Mode from Donne to Cowley* and *The Cavalier Mode from*

Jonson to Cotton) have been published. They make clear (as will the theoretical study) my profound agreement with the central ideas of Professor Alpers' paper. The third study, *The Restoration Mode from Donne to Milton* (due for publication later this year) contains a long second part on "The Triumph of Narrative," beginning in the 1640's and going on to the achievements of Butler, Milton, and Dryden. This brief paper constitutes, then, an interim attempt to combine theoretical and historical preoccupations.

Notes

1. *On the Sublime,* IX, 9.

2. *The Lives of the English Poets,* ed. G. B. Hill, 3 vols. (Oxford: Clarendon Press, 1905), I, 175.

3. *Lives,* I, 189. In *Rambler,* no. 139, Johnson said: "nothing passes between the first act and the last, that either hastens or delays the death of Sampson" (*The Works of Samuel Johnson,* vol. IV, ed. W. J. Bate and Albrecht B. Strauss [New Haven and London: Yale University Press, 1969], p. 376).

4. *Rambler,* no. 139; *Works,* IV, 371.

5. Else, *Aristotle's Poetics: The Argument* (Cambridge, Mass.: Harvard University Press, 1967).

6. Aristotle's definition implies a pluralistic concept, middles, and he sometimes (*e.g.,* XXIII. 59a. 20) says as much: ἀρχὲυ καὶ ΜΕΣΑ καὶ τέλος (my stress). His usages of the three terms sometimes approximate English meanings, but "beginning" often means something more like "first cause" and "ending" something more like "fulfillment."

7. Else, pp. 284–85. See n. 16 below.

8. Müller, in *Festschrift Paul Kluckhohn und Herman Schneider* (Tübingen; J. C. B. Mohr, 1948), pp. 195–212, a highly stimulating discussion. See also Eberhard Lämmert, *Bauformen des Erzählens,* 2nd printing (Stuttgart: Metzler, 1967).

9. *Gondibert,* II, v–vi.

10. See Davenant, "Preface" to *Gondibert,* ed. David F. Gladish (Oxford: Clarendon Press, 1971), ll. 506–23. The history of the analogy is discussed by Richard H. Perkinson, "The Epic in Five Acts," *Studies in Philology,* XLIII (1946), 465–81.

11. See Hobbes's "Answer" to Davenant's "Preface" in *Gondibert,* ed. Gladish, pp. 45–46.

12. In his excellent book, Lämmert (see note 8) very usefully discusses narrative under the three heads of retrospection, concatenation, and foreshadowing, with views more subtle than conventions of *in medias res.*

13. Cf. also *Beowulf* and *Troilus and Crisyde.* The medieval dream vision for longish poems employs a framing device rather than the convention of beginning in middle things. To the already long list may be added the major poems of Dante, Ariosto, Tasso, and Camões.

14. Dryden, "Preface" to *Fables* in *Of Dramatic Poesy and Other Critical Essays,* ed. George Watson, 2 vols. (London: Dent, 1962), II, 274–75.

15. Alison T. Higgins, in *Schweizer anglistische Arbeiten,* XXXI, (Bern, 1953), 9–10.

16. It will be clear that I regard "movement" not as a property of a literary text but of the process of a mind engaged in reading and understanding a text.

II

Mode in Narrative Poetry

PAUL ALPERS

IN THIS PAPER, I want to analyze the meaning and argue for the importance of the critical term "mode." Critics resort to this term and use it in crucial places, because it uniquely fuses formal and thematic considerations. It is the term to use when we want to suggest that the ethos of a work informs its technique and that techniques imply an ethos. Hence one critic writes an article on "The Augustan Mode in English Poetry"[1]—not the Augustan style or ethos. Another writes on "The Comic Mode of *Measure for Measure*"[2]—not the comic style or form or structure or vision. When Helen Vendler, in her fine study of Wallace Stevens, wants to point out the difference between the so-called thought of a poem and the poem itself, she says, "Such a paraphrase of the poem does not reveal its mode."[3] Robert Garis uses "mode" when he wants a single word to indicate the basic subject of his *The Dickens Theatre*— a book which concerns not style or characterization or dramaturgy or symbolism taken by themselves, but the human implications and dimensions of all these as they exist in whole novels.[4]

Clearly "mode" is felt to be a powerful and comprehensive term. Yet, with one notable exception, there has been no theoretical discussion of it, and of the many writers who use it, hardly one defines it. The word does not appear in the Preminger-Warnke *Dictionary of Poetry and Poetics*. You will not find a definition of "mode" in Josephine Miles' *Eras and Modes in English Poetry* or in Angus Fletcher's *Allegory: The Theory of a Symbolic Mode* or in Earl Miner's two books on seventeenth-century poetry, *The Metaphysical Mode* and *The Cavalier Mode*. Indeed, what seems remarkable about the word is that it can be used reliably and with great resonance, even without prior definition. Hence the purpose of this paper is less to correct or modify the *ad hoc* uses of the term than to explain and justify them. As an epigraph in Richard's *Practical Criticism* has it, "Let us get closer to the fire and see what we are saying."

To begin, I want to put aside two uses of "mode" that are related to, but not the same as, its use as a critical term. The first is the musical term "mode," which in both Greek and Church music refers to a diatonic scale that is selected out of a larger set of possibilities. Each mode was supposed to have certain inherent characteristics which gave rise to certain predictable emotional effects in the listener: hence one writer defines "mode" as an "ethically informed musical pattern."[5] This suggests interesting parallels with the critical term, but we must remember that they are simply parallels; no modern critic who uses "mode" thinks of himself as adopting the musical term.

"Mode" as a critical term should also be distinguished from its very common use in such phrases as "modes of being," "modes of understanding," and "modes of imitation." In such usages, the word never stands alone: it always occurs in the formula "mode of *x*." Its grammar thus directly reflects its meaning: "a particular form, manner, or variety (of some quality, process, or condition)" (*OED*). The quality, process, or condition of which the thing is a mode must always be specified.

By contrast, the critical term stands independently, and we must now ask what it means. Fortunately, the one treatment of the term is full of insight and suggestion. This is the first chapter of Northrop Frye's *Anatomy of Criticism,* entitled "Historical Criticism: Theory of Modes." Frye begins by saying:

26

In literary fictions the plot consists of somebody doing something. The somebody, if an individual, is the hero, and the something he does or fails to do is what he can do, or could have done, on the level of the postulates made about him by the author and the consequent expectations of the audience. Fictions, therefore, may be classified, not morally, but by the hero's power of action, which may be greater than ours, less, or roughly the same.[6]

He then goes on to specify five modes—myth, romance, high mimetic (epic and tragedy), low mimetic (comedy and the novel), and ironic—according to the hero's stature in relation to other men and to the environment of other men. Frye himself never tells us why he calls these categories "modes." But we can find an explanation in Angus Fletcher's wonderfully illuminating comment on Frye's term. "The term 'mode' is appropriate because in each of the five the hero is a protagonist with a given strength relative to his world, and as such each hero—whether mythic, romantic, high mimetic, low mimetic, or ironic—is a *modulor* for verbal architectonics; man is the measure, the *modus* of myth."[7]

From Fletcher's remark, I want to develop a more adequate definition of "mode." But first, what is inadequate about Frye's use of the term? Exactly what is inadequate about all his criticism, brilliant and enlivening though it is: he treats literature and literary works as closed systems. He therefore does not account for what is of the essence in ordinary and *ad hoc* uses of the term "mode"—the sense of the way the mind grasps, assesses, contemplates, and relates itself to all the human and natural phenomena that the work in question presents. Frye of course recognizes that a literary work is the manifestation of a single intelligence and makes its appeal to another intelligence. "There can hardly be a work of literature," he says, "without some kind of relation implied or expressed, between its creator and its auditors."[8] But Frye's account of this relation is very unsatisfactory. At one point he says, very suggestively, that "cer-

27

tain standards of normality common to author and reader are assumed."[9] But it turns out that he thinks this is true only in the low mimetic mode—that is, when the hero and world of the work are exactly like us and our world. In the other modes, he tends to give the poet the human stature of the hero and leaves the reader sitting in his armchair, still *l'homme moyen sensuel.*[10] We can fit Shakespeare writing for the groundlings into this scheme of things, but not Milton writing for a "fit audience." Frye never explores the sense in which *any* work implies its audience. It never occurs to him that his phrase about "certain standards of normality common to author and reader" might be a general truth about mode.

"Mode" is so powerful and trustworthy a term because it suggests the presence of unifying attitudes and sensibility in and behind literary techniques and conventions. As a practical critic, Frye knows about this as well as anyone, but as a theoretician he cannot get it steadily in view. The weakness of his large theoretical structures is revealed by a single sentence: "As soon as the poet's personality appears on the horizon, a relation with the reader is established which cuts across the story."[11] Frye sets up an opposition between completely impersonal narrative and the appearance of the poet's personality. He leaves no room for the figure who is so rightly, if boringly, familiar to us—the narrator who is the "I" who tells the story, but who is not identical with the author in real life. By the same token, Frye treats the relation with the reader as "cutting across" the story, which therefore is assumed to have an independent existence of its own, as if it were a real concatenation of events. Frye of course goes on to say that no work of literature is pure fiction, but the fact is that the sharp and naive dichotomy suggested by this sentence becomes the basis of his largest theoretical division— that between fictional and thematic modes. The latter category includes all works, like didactic epics and lyric poems, in which the writer impresses his own world view, mind, or voice on the reader.

In Frye's treatment of mode, plot and thought, Aristotle's *mythos* and *dianoia,* are regarded as separate, antithetical, and ultimate categories. Along with them go the following pairs of opposites: Aristotle vs. Longinus, objective vs. subjective, catharsis vs. response. These antithetical pairs are of the very essence of Frye's writing and thinking. We do not stop to object as we read, because he is always moving from one to the other, playing them off against each other or intimating their harmonies. But his prose, for all its energy and subtlety, crystallizes out into fixed dichotomies. In this particular list of opposites, he has left a no-man's-land between the terms in each pair, an uncharted territory between distance and absorption, between objective and subjective, in which lies a great deal of what interests us as critics and readers. Poetic narrative lies almost wholly in this unmapped territory; using Frye's terms, we can only say that any poetic narrative will be some combination of fictional and thematic modes.[12] But if we transfer Frye's definition of mode to the poet's and reader's relation to a work, I think we shall have a concept that is direct and unforced in application and powerful in implication.

The definition I have in mind is this: mode is the literary manifestation, in a given work, of the writer's and the putative reader's assumptions about man's nature and situation. As a critical concept, this definition provides a question we should put to all works: what notions of man's strength, possibilities, pleasures, dilemmas, etc., are manifested in the emphases, the devices, the organization, the pleasures, etc., of this work? We can now rephrase Fletcher's remark in the following way: "The term 'mode' is appropriate because the poet or reader is conceived as having a given strength relative to his world and the world of the poem; hence he is a *modulor* for verbal architectonics; man is the measure, the *modus,* of myth." However, it would be very misleading to scrutinize a work and arrange its details in order to get a neat answer to the question, "What is the mode of this work?" Rather, I think it much truer to say that when you engage in normal interpretation you will find that you have implicitly been engaged with this question. This would explain why "mode" so often appears as a powerful summarizing term, but is almost never defined analytically, as if to be applied. I therefore want to explore the significance of the term by showing its relevance to two classical problems of interpretation in Renaissance poetry—Guyon's destruction of the Bower of Bliss, in Book II of *The Faerie Queene,* and the internal monologue, in Book IX of *Paradise Lost,* in which Adam decides to join Eve in her fall.

II

Here is the stanza in which Guyon destroys the Bower of Bliss:

> But all those pleasant bowres and Pallace braue,
> *Guyon* broke downe, with rigour pittilesse;
> Ne ought their goodly workmanship might saue
> Them from the tempest of his wrathfulnesse,
> But that their blisse he turn'd to balefulnesse:
> Their groues he feld, their gardins did deface,
> Their arbers spoyle, their Cabinets suppresse,
> Their banket houses burne, their buildings race,
> And of the fairest late, now made the fowlest place.[13]

Why is the problem this stanza presents a problem of mode? First and most obviously, because qualities of writing and experience are at issue, and it is for these that critics tend to invoke the word "mode." The severity with which Spenser renders Guyon's action is in sharp contrast to the seductiveness of the Bower itself. Critics who feel something has gone wrong here do so because they feel a sudden shift in the quality of the writing, a shift which they find unjustifiable in terms of the canto itself and unacceptable in its implicit views of human nature. Conversely, Guyon's action could be justified by arguing, with C. S. Lewis, that the quality of experience in the Bower is consistently sterile and repugnant. Whatever view we take of the canto will be an argument about its mode—that is, to return to our definition, about the literary manifestations of the writer's and reader's assumptions about man's nature and situation. And we shall see, I hope, how useful it is to approach questions of mode by the specific notion—which underlies the connection between *modus* as manner and *modus* as measure—of man's strength relative to his world.

Not only Lewis but many of his opponents assume that in the Bower of Bliss Spenser could not have intended us to feel the tensions which most of us in fact do feel when we read this canto. Yet from the very beginning, Spenser makes it clear that such tensions are of the essence of human experience. In the opening episode, he establishes a pattern for all the subsequent renderings of the trials of temperance. In this episode, Guyon and the Palmer pass in their boat between the Gulf of Greediness and the Rock of Vile Reproach—moralized versions of Scylla and Charybdis, as the whole canto is a moralized version of the *Odyssey*. Before reaching these twin perils, the Boatman describes them to Guyon and the Palmer in two vivid stanzas (3-4). However, when the boat arrives on the spot, we are given four more stanzas (5-8) of even more powerful description of the gulf and the rock. Finally, when the boat has passed through, the Palmer gives a moral interpretation (st. 9), even though both the Boatman's forewarning and the poet's direct description have been full of moral significance. We have, then, a clear pattern of anticipating, enduring, and understanding a spiritual danger. We can see that Milton was interpreting his master truly, when he praised this canto for showing the dependence of moral knowledge on experience and trial.

The subsequent episodes of the canto can be seen as developing and complicating the simple pattern established by this first one. In the sea voyage that occupies the first half of the

31

canto, the increasing complexity of this pattern of moral encounter is achieved by the following devices: surprises and other complications of the Boatman's warnings, as when the maiden calling for help turns out *not* to be the anticipated siren;[14] Guyon's innocent but dangerous impulses to help damsels in distress or listen to attractive melodies (st. 28, 33); and the transformation of the Palmer's moralizations from mere commentaries to direct acts of rejection or of keeping the boat on its course (st. 16, 26). Moral understanding now tends to take the form of moral choice, and after Guyon and the Palmer land in Acrasia's realm, the pattern of anticipation, full experience, and understanding becomes a pattern of externalized narration and action. The ivory gateway to Acrasia's realm, with its depiction of Jason and Medea's destructive love, is analogous to the foreknowledge the Boatman had provided. We then meet Genius, and Guyon, having absorbed the Palmer's severity, overturns his bowl of wine and breaks his magic staff. We next enter an idyllic landscape, and by comparison with the preceding episode—where we encountered an artifact, not nature—what is morally suspicious is more diffused through and merged with what is attractive and, it seems, humanly valuable. By the same token, the description of Excess and her bower, which immediately follows, is more powerfully engaging than the description of Genius. We indubitably see Excess for what she is, but the issue, as Milton knew, is how the whole spirit confronts and endures her pressures. Hence, whereas Guyon overturned Genius' bowl "disdainfully," he breaks Excess' cup "violently" (st. 49, 57). From these summaries, you will see that Guyon's vehement destruction of the Bower is not a unique action to which all has been tending, but coming as it does after the most alluring descriptions in the canto, the last instance of the pattern seen in these two earlier episodes—which themselves are developments of the pattern of episodes in the sea voyage.

32

I think it is clear that we have been discussing the mode of this canto. For one thing, we have been talking about what we would call, in conversation, the way the poem works, and "mode" is a good written equivalent for this perhaps too casual phrase. Moreover, we have been talking about mode as we have technically defined it. Milton's praise in *Areopagitica* makes it clear that the literary techniques of the canto are based on a view of "man's strength relative to his world."

Assuredly we bring not innocence into the world, we bring impurity much rather: that which purifies us is triall, and triall is by what is contrary. That vertue therefore which is but a youngling in the contemplation of evill, and knows not the utmost that vice promises to her followers, and rejects it, is but a blank vertue, not a pure; her whitenesse is but an excrementall whitenesse; Which was the reason why our sage and serious Poet *Spencer,* whom I dare be known to think a better teacher than *Scotus* or *Aquinas,* describing true temperance under the person of *Guion,* brings him in with his palmer through the cave of Mammon, and the bowr of earthly blisse that he might see and know, and yet abstain.[15]

Finally, the concept of mode brings into focus one further problem: what is the status of the actions which conclude these episodes? The orthodox interpretation of the canto takes Guyon's destruction of the Bower to be a unique and definitive action; it resolves all moral issues, and all moral values inhere in it. But it is precisely this view that creates critical difficulties, because Spenser makes no bones of the fact that Guyon's destruction is wrathful and pitiless. Yet two stanzas after he wrecks the bower, Guyon is wonderfully generous to and pitying of Acrasia's victims. Either Spenser is confused, or he does not think the destruction itself sufficiently renders man's resolution of the spiritual issues posed by Acrasia. The pattern we have described in the canto shows that the latter is the case, because Spenser makes us see that no single act of rejection is unique and defining; rather, our spiritual life is a continual sequence of experiences and choices. This view explains Spenser's rendering of the sea voyage, in which he calls attention on five separate occasions to the unflagging energy with which the Boatman rows along.[16] Similarly, formulas like "Forward they passe" occur some dozen times,[17] because Guyon and the Palmer pass the various tests of choice and endurance not in order to settle issues definitively, but to keep on their steady course. Hence the canto ends with the Palmer acknowledging the moral dilemmas posed by Grill and summoning Guyon once more to his journey: "Let *Grill* be *Grill,* and haue his hoggish mind, / But let vs hence depart, whilest wether serues and wind."

Having shown that Guyon's destruction of the Bower is consonant with the workings of the rest of the canto, we must return to the problem with which we began—the particular quality of the stanza which renders that action. It is here particularly that we must extend Frye's concept of mode to include the reader. What we have seen so far could have been discerned by applying Frye's notions of the internal workings of a fiction. But only by directly attending to the reader can we give a positive account, a critical justification, of the poetic severity of that stanza, the way it enforces the phrase "rigour pittilesse."

We can begin to justify the stanza by pointing out that, throughout Book II, man's spiritual strength involves the very energies and forces that he seeks to control. Thus Guyon's aroused anger gives him strength to fight Furor and Pyrochles;[18] he is courteous when he resists Phaedria's blandishments;[19] immediately after disdaining Mammon's treasures with "bold mesprise," he meets the giant Disdain, who embodies this particular characteristic.[20] When Guyon smashes the cup of Excess, his violence is the heroic counterpart of Excess' reaction: "Whereas *Excesse* exceedingly was wroth" (st.57). The repetition of this motif in Book II is due to Spenser's steady contemplation of a truth of which the major emblems are Guyon's faint after

34

enduring Mammon's trial and Arthur's wounded, exhausted condition after his battle with Maleger[21]—that man's moral strength, when conceived as heroic and autonomous, has inherent limits and inescapably takes its toll of the human spirit. The frank portrayal of Guyon's destructive energies makes this point once more, and it is clear that his rigor and wrath are reactions to what Acrasia threatens—dissipation in the fullest sense. But the narrative in this stanza is markedly externalized, an effect increased by the formulaic listing in the final lines. We therefore do not feel the emotional forces at work, in the way we do when Guyon is "exceeding wroth" at a blow from Pyrochles or prepares to battle Disdain. To adapt Helen Vendler's remark about Stevens, we cannot fall back on paraphrase. If we are to stay in touch with the details of Spenser's rendering and the quality of our experience in reading—for the counterpart of "How does it work?" is "What is it like to read?"—we must talk about the way our minds engage, take in, apprehend the truths and phenomena presented.

We have so far described the patterns of the Bower of Bliss canto as more or less direct renderings of psychological experience. Spenser is not a dramatic writer in the ordinary sense, but we have talked as if the effect of his verse is to make us experience in ourselves what the characters experience in the allegorical fiction. But this ignores an essential characteristic of this canto—the repeated externalizing of phenomena into static, morally significant descriptions, for which the best single term is "emblematic." The canto is of course filled with emblematic settings—like the Rock of Vile Reproach, the Quicksand of Unthriftyhead, and the fountain with its metal ivy—and emblematic characters, like Phaedria and Excess. But the emblematic tendency also affects the rendering of action. Thus the transition between the sea voyage and the entry into the Bower of Bliss is the Palmer's taming Acrasia's beasts with his magical staff, made of the same wood as Mercury's caduceus (st. 40-41).

35

Because of the emblematic tendency in the writing, moral mastery in this canto appears not solely as achieved conquest or endurance of trial, as it does in the Cave of Mammon, but also as the conscious knowledge that emerges from such experience. It sounds as if we should be speaking of "distance" here, but that word can be misleading. The descriptions of the bathing girls, of Acrasia's music, and of Acrasia herself are as "close" as anything in Spenser. Conversely, there is much moral argument and reflection in the Cave of Mammon. But between the two cantos there are important differences in Guyon's relation to his experience and our relation to Guyon. The Cave of Mammon begins with a debate in which Guyon is a conscious spokesman for all mankind, and in Mammon's realm he directly encounters every significant emblem. He is central and prominent up to the very end of the canto, when he rejects Tantalus' plea, takes a long look at the tormented Pilate, and resists the temptation to eat from Proserpina's tree. Spenser does not render everything by means of Guyon's experience, but at any given moment Guyon can be a surrogate for the reader. In canto xii, on the other hand, our self-knowledge lies less in the shared experience of the hero's encounters than in contemplated images and patterns of experience, of which the hero is only a part. Thus our image of man at the beginning of the canto is not the autonomous hero, but a trio of figures who are an emblem of the composite soul. Guyon cannot be our surrogate here, and as the canto proceeds the reader more and more becomes the human center of the episode.

By the end of the canto, when *our* minds are expanding to experience and include more and more, Guyon and the Palmer are increasingly reduced. Thus the last incident of moral anticipation in the canto does not occur to the characters at all, but only to the reader. As Guyon and the Palmer approach the Bower, they hear "a most melodious sound, / Of all that mote delight a daintie eare" (st. 70). After two ravishing stanzas, Spenser says:

> There, whence that Musick seemed heard to bee,
> Was the faire Witch her selfe now solacing,
> With a new Louer. (72)

There follows a severe and disturbing description of Acrasia gazing on her sleeping lover (st. 73). At this point it is impossible to tell that Guyon and the Palmer have not reached Acrasia. We assume that they have and that they are present when Acrasia's courtiers go on to sing the rose song (st. 74–75). In fact they do not arrive until after the song is ended. Their arrival occasions another description of Acrasia and Verdant, but this time it is erotic, intoxicating, captivating (st. 77–79). Clearly Spenser has made the *reader* undergo the same pattern of anticipated knowledge and full experience that the characters underwent in earlier episodes. Spenser gives no indication of how Guyon and the Palmer react to Acrasia's alluring beauty; by the same token, the grave meditation on Verdant's fate is in the poet's own voice, directed to us (st. 79–80). Guyon and the Palmer are not our surrogates here: they are not represented as having any thoughts at all. We see them in a wider context than they see; we see them from the outside; we see them in action:

> The noble Elfe, and carefull Palmer drew
> So nigh them, minding nought, but lustfull game,
> That suddein forth they on them rusht, and threw
> A subtile net, which onely for the same
> The skilfull Palmer formally did frame. (81)

This is an emblematic action, and not simply because it is a version of Vulcan's capturing Venus and Mars in his net. It is an emblematic rendering of the point we have already discussed: Acrasia must be defeated by valid manifestations of the spiritual powers she corrupts. The Palmer's net is emphatically

37

an artifact, and in calling it "subtle," Spenser makes it literally a strong version of Acrasia's silk and silver veil, of which he says, four stanzas earlier, "More subtle web *Arachne* cannot spin" (st. 77). Where we apprehended Spenser's point in the Cave of Mammon by a sense of sharing Guyon's endurance of his oppressive and nightmarish experience, the image of the Palmer's net makes a similar moral point much more strictly a matter of conscious knowledge.

These points about the rendering of action and our relation to it are equally true of Guyon's destruction of the Bower of Bliss, which immediately follows the description of the capturing of Acrasia. By externalizing and fixing Guyon's devastation of the Bower, Spenser gives the form of conscious knowledge to our awareness of the limitations of action, the costs of heroic autonomy, the severity with which spiritual opposites clash in human experience, and the power of the necessities that reign in the wars of the spirit. If this stanza ended the canto, as Guyon's faint ends canto vii, it might appear to be simply the recommended action that vulgar notions of didacticism assume it is. But Spenser beautifully places it in relation to man's whole nature and moral experience when he turns to the generous and steadfast freeing of Acrasia's victims, now "comely men" but still feeling shame, even wrath and resentment. As we go beyond it in this way, Guyon's destruction of the Bower becomes a true piece of self-knowledge for us, as we understand, acknowledge, and endure its bitter severity.

There is no mystery about why the Cave of Mammon and the Bower of Bliss differ as they do. The reader's relation to the two cantos closely parallels the hero's role in each. All Spenser has done in the final episode of the Bower of Bliss is transfer to us the powers he gave his human triad in the first episode— of anticipating, experiencing and enduring, and interpreting a spiritually significant encounter. Why then do we not simply describe the internal workings of a poem—what Frye calls fictional modes—and extrapolate from them? Because this involves too strict a commitment to the notion of autonomous fictions, of works as closed systems. Too much is then excluded, so that as practical critics we find ourselves without a positive interpretation of Guyon's final action and as theoreticians we find ourselves in Frye's position of having to devise an entire separate structure of thematic modes. But if we do not think of the reader's mind as a *tabula rasa* for taking the impression of the fictional modes, if, on the contrary, we think of ourselves as being, along with the poet and hero, the measure of the myth in question, then the two elements that are artificially separated as fictional and thematic come together in a powerful unifying concept.

III

Adam's decision to join Eve in her fall is perhaps the most difficult interpretive problem in a poem full of such problems. Within the scope of this paper, I cannot hope to establish decisively the interpretation I offer. But I hope it will be clear that, whatever interpretation is offered, questions about mode will underlie it. The problem about Adam's internal monologue, as everyone knows, is that it is full of emotional power and human appeal, while at the same time it assents to bringing death into the world and all our woe. We feel immense sympathy with Adam, and yet know he is doing something wrong; Frye neatly describes this as a clash between the dramatic and the conceptual.[22] The orthodox view of this clash is that Adam should not have been victimized by it: he knew what he was about to do was wrong, he should have resisted his feelings, and trusted in God to work something out. But as this argument appears, for example, in Lewis' *Preface to "Paradise Lost,"* it tends to diminish the power of Adam's monologue or simply ignore its literary character. This defect is repaired in the affective criticism of Stanley Fish, who argues that we are meant to feel the power of Adam's monologue, but nevertheless are to

39

judge against him. Fish regards *Paradise Lost* as a series of tests of the reader, which he calls "good temptations"; interpreting Adam's monologue is our supreme test, just as the decision itself is Adam's.[23] Clearly Fish has a strong sense of mode, though he does not use the term. His book is distinguished by its full and rigorous working out of the human implications of the way *Paradise Lost* works, stylistically and structurally. Hence, in supporting his readings, Fish continually and explicitly appeals to what he regards as the views of Milton and seventeenth-century Christianity on "man's strength relative to his world."

I want to argue that Fish and Lewis and many other critics are wrong to say that Adam should have decided not to eat the apple and join Eve—or rather are wrong in the way they say it, for criticism too has its modes. Let us begin with a traditional problem of mode, the relation of Book IX to tragic drama, the form in which many Renaissance writers (including Milton himself at one time) conceived the Fall of Man. When we look at seventeenth-century tragedies about the Fall, we find their treatment of Adam's fall is quite unlike Milton's.[24] In every one of these plays, Adam at first refuses to accept the apple from Eve; a full argument ensues, in which Adam explicitly says that obedience to God has first claim on him; Eve repeatedly appeals to and plays on his love and fear of loneliness, and finally half lures, half forces him to yield. In this mode, the conflict in Adam's loyalties is explicit, and his motive for eating the apple is clearly unworthy of him. There is no doubt in any of these plays that Adam and his descendents reading his tragedy should and *could* choose God over Woman and Nature. In the scene in *Paradise Lost,* by contrast, there is no debate, argument, or internal conflict. Adam's dismay on hearing of Eve's sin immediately produces the internal monologue in which he decides to join her. We hear nothing of his obligations to God, only of his resolution in this crisis. It will be argued that Milton's point is that Adam does ignore God, but

the debate about this passage is precisely whether the dramaturgy and the verse enforce this awareness on our part. In other
words, any interpretive argument has to make or imply, as Fish
does, an argument about mode. At this crucial moment, are
we made to feel that Adam's strength relative to his world and
ours to ours are such that a different choice could and should
have been made?

We can investigate Adam's strength relative to his world by
asking what is the status of the impulse on which he acts at this
moment. It is no derogation of him to say that he acts on impulse, for he is still in a state of innocence, and his feelings are
still in harmony with nature. But what does this mean in that
small stretch of time—which does not exist in the Biblical account—between Eve's fall and Adam's? When Eve eats the
apple, Milton says

> Earth felt the wound, and nature from her seat
> Sighing through all her works gave signs of woe,
> That all was lost.[25]

The question of Adam's strength is precisely whether he is in-
cluded in the works of nature which all feel this wound. He
himself says, "I feel the link of nature draw me" (9.914).
Those who argue that he can reject Eve and that therefore all
was *not* lost assume that his powers transcend nature and its
bonds and imperatives. Let us see what Milton tells us when
he returns to Adam, awaiting Eve's return:

> Great joy he promised to his thoughts, and new
> Solace in her return, so long delayed;
> Yet oft his heart, divine of something ill,
> Misgave him; he the faltering measure felt.   (9.843–846)

The "faltering measure" is the motions of Adam's heart. But
the deictic force of "the" and the syntactic parallel of the two
noun phrases, "something ill" and "faltering measure," enforce
the reference to an external event, the general wound felt by

41

nature's works. By making "he the faltering measure felt" a separate clause, with no explanatory conjunction, Milton poises it between internal feelings and the external events indicated by the preceding clause. He thus makes us apprehend, in the intimacy and fullness of our reading, that Adam's forebodings are completely in touch with reality. It is one of the most compelling moments in the poem, and Milton confirms its significance when Adam's dismay at Eve's sin produces the fading of the roses in the garland he made for Eve (9.888–893). In the face of this, how can we say that Adam is wrong to feel the imperatives that determine his decision?

> Some cursed fraud
> Of enemy hath beguiled thee, yet unknown
> *And me with thee hath ruined,* for with thee
> Certain my resolution is to die;
> How can I live without thee, how forgo
> Thy sweet converse and love so dearly joined,
> To live again in *these wild woods forlorn?*
>
> (9.904–910, my italics)

I spoke of the line about "the faltering measure" as compelling, and surely this is the word the common reader would use about Adam's monologue. But its validity is purely aesthetic. As a matter of theology, Milton would have rejected the notion that Adam was in any sense compelled to eat the forbidden fruit. So we find ourselves back at the heart of the controversy, with critics like Waldock telling us that "we should allow no one, *not even Milton,* to prise us loose" from the effect of Adam's words,[28] and orthodox Miltonists quoting *De Doctrina Christiana* and other theological texts. We find that it is not sufficient to consider Adam taken by himself. We must directly consider how our own minds apprehend this moment and its human meaning. In a poem on this subject, narrating this event, is it possible that we can read poetically and not theologically? I think that it is—that is, that Milton wrote in such a way that

42

he could avoid, for example, the question, which necessarily concerned commentators on Genesis, of whether the fall occurred when Eve ate the apple or not until Adam did.[27] If we read the phrase "all was lost" the way theologians read the Bible, it seems to commit Milton to the view that Eve's fall was Man's fall. But the parallel passage, when Adam eats the apple, shows that Milton means to beg this particular question:

> Nature gave a second groan,
> Sky loured and muttering thunder, some sad drops
> Wept at *completing of the mortal sin*
> Original. (9.1001–04, my italics)

But we are still left with the question: if the phrase "all was lost" does not entail a theological commitment of the ordinary sort, how can it have the poetic force that it does?

The answer lies, I think, in the relation Milton establishes between the reader and the events of this book of the poem. Throughout the poem, Milton assumes a fallen reader (how could he not?), and it is by now widely recognized that he continually exploits and appeals to the reader's condition. But this does not mean that the reader has a fixed relation to the events of the poem. Consider two interventions of the poet's voice, one from Book IV, the other from Book IX. At the end of the "Hail wedded love" passage, Milton says:

> Sleep on
> Blest pair; and O yet happiest if ye seek
> No happier state, and know to know no more. (4.773–775)

When Eve leaves Adam to garden alone and promises to return at noon, he says:

> O much deceived, much failing, hapless Eve,
> Of thy presumed return! Event perverse!
> Thou never from that hour in Paradise
> Found'st either sweet repast, or sound repose. (9.404–407)

Both passages are full of pathos, because both appeal to our

43

sense of the fragility of the state of innocence. But in Book IV, Milton speaks as if Adam and Eve can maintain themselves in their happy state; the lines in Book IX are spoken in the full knowledge that they did not. This suggests something about Adam's and Eve's strength relative to their world in these two books, but does not settle the issue of ours. For example, a conservative Miltonist might argue that Milton's words in Book IX reproach Eve—rightly sensing that if we speak of pathos here, we acknowledge the limitations of our own strength. I do not know that one could settle the issue on the basis of these lines alone. But it is certainly the case that in Book IX, in contrast with earlier books, Eve exists in an atmosphere of pathos. It manifests itself in her speeches, as when she says, "Frail is our happiness, if this be so, / And Eden were no Eden thus exposed" (340); in her actions, as when she naively follows Satan; in the poet's comments, as when he calls her "fairest unsupported flower, / From her best prop so far, and storm so nigh" (432); and even in the reactions of Satan, who is momentarily "with rapine sweet bereaved" of his fierceness when he sees her (461).

The strain of pathos in Book IX is an implicit manifestation of something we can establish in direct terms: that as compared with Book IV, both poet and reader are represented as diminished in strength relative to their world. Compare the poet himself in the opening lines of each book. In Book IV, he speaks in urgent, prophetic tones, as if caught up in the illusion that Adam and Eve might yet escape Satan:

> O for that warning voice, which he who saw
> The Apocalypse, heard cry in heaven aloud,
> Then when the dragon, put to second rout,
> Came furious down to be revenged on men,
> *Woe to the inhabitants on earth!* that now,
> While time was, our first parents had been warned
> The coming of their secret foe, and scaped
> Haply so scaped his mortal snare.   (4.1–8)

In Book IX, the tone is more down to earth, occasionally brusque, and the poet speaks out of constraint:

> No more of talk where God or angel guest
> With man, as with his friend, familiar used
> To sit indulgent, and with him partake
> Rural repast, permitting him the while
> Venial discourse unblamed: I now must change
> Those notes to tragic.   (9.1–6)

By the same token, Milton's self-portrait in this opening passage is stripped of heroic aspects; his inspiration is less fully felt and rendered than elsewhere in the poem; his Muse is uniquely represented as having a quite external relation to him. He will succeed, he says,

> unless an age too late, or cold
> Climate, or years damp my intended wing
> Depressed, and much they may, if all be mine,
> Not hers who brings it nightly to my ear.   (9.44–47)

In the case of the reader, it is the heroic similes that most explicitly show his relation to the events of this book. Take the passage that follows the description of Eve among her roses:

> Spot more delicious than those gardens feigned
> Or of revived Adonis, or renowned
> Alcinous, host of old Laertes' son,
> Or that, not mystic, where the sapient king
> Held dalliance with his fair Egyptian spouse.   (9.439–443)

These similes have a particular character that belongs to Book IX. In Book IV, Eden is compared to later gardens and land-scapes in order that we may apprehend, from our present knowledge and powers, the original state of innocence. The rationale of this poetic effort is like the view that pagan myths were intimations of Christian truth, so that Hesperian fables are "if true, here only." The characteristic movement in Book IV is indicated by the description of Eden (4.235–68), which

45

begins with poetic diffidence—"but rather to tell how, if art could tell"—and ends with so strong a manifestation of creative powers that Milton brings into the Garden of Eden Pan and the Graces and Hours of classical mythology.[28] By the same token, the list of gardens which cannot be compared to Eden is done with such scholarly, mythical, sensory, and rhetorical energy and sweep that Milton can proceed without a pause from it to our first sight of Adam and Eve. He is so in command of his and our resources that he can place Satan in a subordinate clause that specifies his incapacity to feel the delights we do (4.285). But in these lines in Book IX, he is brief and restrained. The noblest human imaginings, the gardens of Adonis and Alcinous, are sharply characterized as "feigned," while the real garden is that of Solomon, enacting a severely moral interpretation of the fall of man. To call Solomon "the sapient king" increases the moral stringency, for it represents him at his noblest and employs a word that is notorious for having a harmonious double meaning before the fall and a problematic one after it. Both the rhetorical manner of these lines and the nature of the allusions have the effect of putting fallen man, the poet and the reader, on the other side of the gulf that is fixed between Eden and our present world. This rendering of our situation is confirmed as the passage continues:

> Much he the place admired, the person more.
> As one who long in populous city pent,
> Where houses thick and sewers annoy the air,
> Forth issuing on a summer's morn to breathe
> Among the pleasant villages and farms
> Adjoined, from each thing met conceives delight,
> The smell of grain, or tedded grass, or kine,
> Or dairy, each rural sight, each rural sound;
> If chance with nymph-like step fair virgin pass,
> What pleasing seemed, for her now pleases more,
> She most, and in her look sums all delight.   (9.444-454)

What is striking about this simile is not simply that it draws on the everyday world, but that it is confined to it. It lacks the aura or resonance—the capacity to extend our apprehensions to diabolical, divine, or unfallen realities—that characterize other similes, even ones (like the superstitious peasant at 1.780–88) that are based on more disturbing or more ambiguous phenomena. Milton here limits our enchantment with Eden and with Eve to what remains of their original nature in the world as we know it.

Much of what I am saying needs more detailed justification, and my argument as a whole needs a more thorough survey of the similes—and much else—in Book IX. But my purpose here, as I said, is to sketch an argument in order to show the issues that any interpretation must engage. Therefore let me now state the general significance of what I have suggested about our relation to events in Book IX. It seems to me that almost all the dilemmas readers and critics feel in Book IX come from assuming that we follow it in the manner of an ordinary narration of events. Poet, character, and reader are thought to exist at the same moment of time, so that questions like "What next?" or "Why did that happen?" occur to them in more or less the same way. Obviously we know that the fall is going to occur as Adam and Eve do not, but the usual way of interpreting this is as a foreshadowing—the observer's analogue to the foreboding that Adam feels. By the same token, the usual way of treating a simile like the one about Solomon is to call it proleptic—foreshadowing the fall and its consequences. It seems to me that Milton has done something very different from this, something much more mysterious and sublime. All the details we have examined show that we are not moving with the action of the poem—as we inherently would if this were a drama—but are rather contemplating it from a fixed position, on the other side of the events that are unfolding. We know what is going to happen, but we are powerless to affect it—

hence the plangency of a phrase like "all was lost" or the heart-breaking effect of describing Adam, weaving his garland for Eve, as if he were already in the fallen world:

> Adam the while
> Waiting desirous her return, had wove
> Of choicest flowers a garland to adorn
> Her tresses, and her rural labours crown,
> As reapers oft are wont their harvest queen.   (9.838–842)

And hence, most importantly, the heroic grandeur of Adam's decision to join Eve in her fall. It is heroic because it recognizes, assents to, and embraces the necessity of things. Its candid, almost naive, grandeur comes from the fact that the acceptance of our lot is represented not as fallen man's self-awareness and sense of limitations, but as innocent Adam's committing himself to the future and to his kind. The decision has such power because it occurs at a unique moment in human history—when man is suspended between a state of innocence and a fallen condition. The gap between Adam and the reader closes here, and we can sense potentialities working in two directions: Adam committing himself to become like us, "bliss or woe," and ourselves enacting our acceptance of life's conditions in the mode of Adam's candid grandeur. Again let me stress that this is not theology. A theologian necessarily follows the Biblical story as an ordinary narrative, with God as plot-maker and Adam and Eve as responsible agents. In Book IX, Milton's extraordinary rhetorical tactics have freed him from these necessities and enabled him and us to contemplate the fall under the aspect of its meaning for Adam's descendants. Hence Adam and Eve's debate about gardening separately is not an oblique way of finding a cause for the fall or of saying Adam and Eve were really fallen already or of assigning responsibility or blame; it directly opens up problems of human freedom, responsibility, autonomy, and dependence. By the same token,

48

Adam's heroic choice renders not simply the responsibility that theology says is his, but that frank and unflinching acceptance of our lot that is of the essence of the tradition in which Milton wrote and of his conception of man.

IV

I want to conclude with some remarks about the implications of what I have said and argued. In the first place, I have not meant to suggest, as some readers and auditors have thought, that critics who use "mode" without defining it are being vague or careless. Quite the contrary, what has impressed me about my own and other critics' use of this term is that it can be used reliably and with great resonance without a clear formal definition. I would say that my analysis of the term and its use would prove to be true of the way in which other critics use the word —or alternatively would define boundaries beyond which the word *would* be vague and not useful. But the ordinary usage of the term, the way it usually appears in critical discourse, has an important lesson for us. I think questions of mode arise most fruitfully as ways of understanding issues that arise in the normal course of interpretation. This implies a view of literary theory very different from that represented by Frye and many other writers. It means that a definition is not to be applied to a work as if it were an experimental tool for classifying or analyzing an object, but should serve to extend and clarify our awareness of what our minds observe, take in, and understand. In defining mode as man's strength relative to his world (and so forth), we are not, then, specifying an attribute to be isolated and classified. Rather, we are providing questions that enable us to understand what we see and, in the words of Richards' great epigraph, to see what we are saying. This is not to substitute mere subjectivity for a falsely conceived objectivity. On the contrary, the point of conceiving theory this way is to maintain our grasp on the connections that exist between works of art and the human mind.

49

This raises questions that are well beyond the scope of this paper. But one specific consequence of this view of literary theory is already implicit in this paper and should certainly be examined. On the one hand, I have not specified the mode of the Bower of Bliss canto or of Book IX of *Paradise Lost* in the sense of providing a characterizing adjective to go with the noun. On the other hand, I have distinguished the modes of these two narrative units from those of other units within the same work. Such minute discriminations and such thorough absorption of theoretical questions into practical criticism might seem to lose touch entirely with the kind of large-scale classifying of literary works that Frye's work represents, and that is, I entirely agree, an essential part of our self-awareness and capacity as readers. However, I think that what the interpretations in this paper exemplify is perfectly consistent and continuous in our understanding with Frye's large categories and discriminations. First, just as a side remark, let me remind you that there is nothing surprising in saying that units within *The Faerie Queene* and *Paradise Lost* differ from each other: it is a commonplace to talk about the encyclopedic character of these poems and their accommodation of a wide range of genres, literary models, styles, and subjects. But this observation is mainly defensive. The important thing to say is that there is no difficulty at all in discriminating the Cave of Mammon from the Bower of Bliss, but in a broader view saying that they have a common mode in comparison with *Orlando Furioso* or with *Gerusalemme Liberata*. Expanding our view, we could go on to talk about what *The Faerie Queene* and *Orlando Furioso* have in common by comparison with *Don Juan* or *The Charterhouse of Parma*—or perhaps we would want to put *Orlando Furioso* in between *The Faerie Queene* and these later works. In making such comparisons and discriminations of mode, we should use generic and other common terms as much as we can. Thus the mode common to the Cave of Mammon and the

Bower of Bliss is allegorical, and it seems just to call *Gerusalemme Liberata* epic in mode and *Orlando Furioso* romantic (or whatever the adjective of "romance" is). Nevertheless, it is essential to recognize that we do not have to provide a categorical name or characterizing adjective for every discrimination of this sort. That way lies Polonius. Frye's work is both an example and a warning in this respect. His best writing encourages us not only to see the continuity of certain fundamental problems, but also, by its dexterity and flexibility, to be able to make fruitful comparisons whether our field of vision is narrow or wide. But at the same time, Frye feels a need to project his theoretical categories as if they were attributes of an order of literature objectively conceived and even of the world itself. In this mode he proliferates terms and categories, and his criticism and criticism influenced by him become like Donne's satiric description of astronomy:

> For of Meridians, and Parallels,
> Man hath weav'd out a net, and this net throwne
> Upon the Heavens, and now they are his owne.
> (*First Anniversary*, 278–80)

Finally, I want to make some remarks about what I have referred to as the connection between works of art and the human mind. Throughout this paper, I have spoken of the poet's and the reader's minds almost interchangeably. If what I have said is on the right track, then we must envisage a much greater degree of parity between writer and reader than we usually do. The tendency to deify the writer is very marked in modern criticism, as is its corollary, the tendency to make critics a priestly caste, interpreting sacred scriptures. Deification is no less decisive when the poet-god is hidden and we are invited to look on his creation, the work itself. Critics as different as Frye, Wimsatt, and R. S. Crane give us no sense of the bonds or likenesses that exist between the mind that created a work and the mind that reads it. (In this respect, American critics differ markedly from the great English critics of this century, like Leavis, Empson, or Lewis.) Hence even when these critics turn their attention to the relationship between work and reader, they see it working in only one direction. The reader is conceived so passively, so much as a mere object of manipulation and field of operation, that he tends to be absorbed into the work itself. Thus the essay on generic criticism in Frye's *Anatomy* is called "rhetorical criticism" on the grounds that "genre is determined by the conditions established between the poet and his public."[20] But Frye simply absorbs this relationship into his objective description of the various genres. The effects of generic structures and devices are seen as inherent in them; hence there is, so to speak, no space to be traversed between work and reader and therefore no sense of a true relation between them—only the effect of a work *on* the reader. The same criticism applies to Wayne Booth's *The Rhetoric of Fiction,* which, despite its title, has been most influential as a tool for analyzing the structures of works and tells us almost nothing about the reader.

Similar liabilities beset what is called "affective criticism," despite its attempt to give the reader his due. The work of Stanley Fish—by all odds the most brilliant and searching of its kind—seems to me simply to turn the assumptions of Frye and Booth upside down. Instead of the work as an object, we have the work as a self-consuming artifact, which exists *only* in the reader's developing responses. The word "response" itself and Fish's insistence on the reader's bondage to a strict moment-by-moment sequential experience are other signs that he regards the reader as essentially passive, the plaything of the work and its author. Where other critics examine the work as the poet's creation, Fish examines the reader as his creature, but he nonetheless views the poet as God. This is explicit not only in his work on *Paradise Lost,* but in his argument that Herbert "makes the experience of his poems the discovery of their true author-

52

ship" (that is, God),[30] and in such splendid remarks as "Pater giveth and Pater taketh away."[31] Fish's view of the reader is explicit in the conclusion of his most important theoretical essay:

Becoming good at the method means asking the question "What does that . . . do?" with more and more awareness of the probable (and hidden) complexity of the answer; that is with a mind more and more sensitized to the workings of language. In a peculiar and unsettling (to theorists) way, it is a method which processes its own user, who is also its only instrument. It is self-sharpening and what it sharpens is *you*. In short, it does not organize materials, but transforms minds.[32]

What is unsettling in these words is not the challenge to theorists, but their human implications. To adapt Whitehead's famous witticism, there is no God and the critic is His prophet. But it is a tricky business, extrapolating social or moral views from a critic's work. To find elitist or hieratic views implicit in Frye seems to me relevant to our current educational dilemmas because they have much to do with Frye's influence. But such extrapolations probably do a good deal of injustice to what Frye personally perceives and thinks. And if his view of literature, or Fish's or anyone else's, is wrong, it is not because it unsettles our feelings or disturbs our self-esteem, but because it is wrong, and the way to show this is in concrete analysis and debate about concrete literary issues.

So I want to conclude by suggesting that in such debates our views of poet and reader will be of the essence, and that we most truly honor a writer not by transfiguring him out of all proportion or likeness to ourselves, but by thinking of him as a man among men, confronting and imagining a common condition, and writing of it in some way, some mode—celebrating, observing, execrating, accepting, whatever. It is this view of writer and reader that underlies a notion of mode and that brings out what the critical term shares, at its deepest level of implication, with the other meanings of the word. The critical term, the musical term, the grammatical term "mood," and the phrase "mode of x" have in common a view of any human act as being a selection from or specific manifestation of a larger reality or set of possibilities that no single act can encompass. As critics we do well to remind ourselves that this is true of the acts of our own minds. Perhaps we should talk less about critical theory and method and more about modes of criticism.

Notes

1. Ralph Cohen, in *Eighteenth-Century Studies,* I (1967), 3–32.

2. Roger Sale, in *Shakespeare Quarterly,* XIX (1968), 55–61.

3. *On Extended Wings* (Cambridge, Mass.: Harvard University Press, 1969), p. 130.

4. "There is a Dickens problem because we ordinarily do not regard the theatrical mode as capable of 'serious' artistic effects and meanings. There is then another mode which does seem capable of these high matters, a mode for which we have no name because it is the only mode which we take 'seriously.'" *The Dickens Theatre* (Oxford: Clarendon Press, 1965), p. 31.

5. John Hollander, *The Untuning of the Sky* (Princeton: University Press, 1961), p. 208.

6. *Anatomy of Criticism* (Princeton: University Press, 1957), p. 33.

7. "Utopian History and the *Anatomy of Criticism,*" in Murray Krieger, ed., *Northrop Frye in Modern Criticism* ("English Institute Essays") (New York: Columbia University Press, 1966), pp. 34–35.

8. *Anatomy,* p. 53.

9. *Ibid.,* p. 49.

10. *Cf.* his definition of "mode" in the Glossary at the end of the *Anatomy:* "A conventional power of action assumed about the chief characters in fictional literature, or the corresponding attitude assumed by the poet toward his audience in thematic literature" (p. 366).

11. *Anatomy,* p. 52.

12. "Every work of literature has both a fictional and a thematic aspect, and the question of which is more important is often simply a matter of opinion or emphasis in interpretation" (*Anatomy,* p. 53).

13. II.xii.83. *The Faerie Queene,* ed. J. C. Smith (Oxford: Clarendon Press, 1909).

14. Stanzas 27–28; *cf.* st. 17 and 30. I first was made aware of the patterns of anticipation and arrival in this canto by a seminar paper by Marcia McClintock Folsom.

15. *Complete Prose Works,* vol. 2, ed. Ernest Sirluck (New Haven: Yale University Press, 1959), pp. 515–16.

16. Stanzas 5, 10, 21, 29, 37.

17. Stanzas 3, 5, 6, 9, 10, 14, 15, 17, 18, 19, 20, 27, 29, 34, 37.

18. iv.9, v.7.

19. vi.21, 26, 36.

20. vii.39–40.

21. vii.66, xi.48–49.

22. *The Return of Eden* (Toronto: University Press, 1965), pp. 83–84.

23. *Surprised by Sin: The Reader in "Paradise Lost"* (New York: St. Martin's Press, 1967), p. 270.

24. These tragedies (and many other analogues to *Paradise Lost*) are collected in Watson Kirkconnell, ed., *The Celestial Cycle* (Toronto: University Press, 1952). The scenes summarized in this paragraph come from the following plays (page numbers are those of the scene of Adam's fall): Hugo Grotius, *Adamus Exul* (1601), pp. 175–85; Giambattista Andreini, *L'Adamo* (1613), pp. 251–57; Serafino della Salandra, *Adamo Caduto* (1647), pp. 326–31; Joost Van den Vondel, *Adam in Ballingschap* (1664), pp. 466–70.

It is interesting that in neither of Milton's two outlines of a tragedy of the Fall (*ca.* 1640, preserved in the Trinity College, Cambridge manuscript) does he provide for a scene or scenes depicting the fall of either Adam or Eve. Modernized transcriptions of these drafts can be found in *A Milton Handbook,* ed. J. H. Hanford and J. G. Taafe (5th edition, New York: Appleton, 1970), pp. 150–53, and *The Poems of Milton,* ed. J. Carey and A. Fowler (London: Longmans, 1968), pp. 419–21.

25. 9.782–84. The text is that of Alastair Fowler (London, 1968) ("Longmans' Annotated English Poets").

26. A. J. A. Waldock, *"Paradise Lost" and Its Critics* (Cambridge: University Press, 1947), p. 47.

27. See Arnold Williams, *The Common Expositor* (Chapel Hill: University of North Carolina Press, 1948), p. 123.

28. For a full discussion of this passage, see my essay, "The Milton Controversy," in *Twentieth-Century Literature in Retrospect,* ed. Reuben A. Brower (Cambridge, Mass., 1971; Harvard English Studies 2), pp. 271–78.

29. *Anatomy,* p. 247.

30. "Letting Go: The Reader in Herbert's Poetry," *ELH,* XXXVII (1970), 478.

31. "Literature in the Reader: Affective Stylistics," *New Literary History,* II (1970), 130.

32. *Ibid.,* 160–61.

III

Sequence and Meaning in Seventeenth-Century Narrative

STANLEY E. FISH

If, AS PAUL RICOEUR has said, "Structuralism is Kantianism without a transcendental subject," then Christianity is structuralism *with* a transcendental subject.[1] This one difference of course finally makes all the difference, but in what they oppose the two systems are very much alike, and what they oppose is what Roland Barthes calls variously "classical language," the ideology of the referent, and, most suggestively, the language of "bad faith." The faith is bad because it is a faith in the innocence and transparency of language, which is in turn a faith in the innocence and transparency of the mind and in its ability to process and elucidate a meaning of which it is independent. To this Barthes and others oppose a view of language which makes it at once more and less, less because it is no longer the privileged conveyer of meaning, more because it becomes, in the true sense of the phrase, meaning-*full*. In this view, meaning is not the product of our operations, but that which makes our operations possible; it does not lie waiting for us at the end of every disposable utterance, but encloses us, includes us, speaks us; and it is the substance and source of all our attempts to apprehend it. "My heart," cries Herbert in *Love II*, "pants thee," rather than pants *after* thee; by deleting the preposition the poet removes the distance between his words and their putative object; that is, he removes the "bad faith

59

attaching to any language which is ignorant of itself" by being ignorant of its origin.[2]

Removing the bad faith is the program of the literature Barthes admires, modern poetry since Mallarmé and the novel since Flaubert, and the distinctive feature of this literature is the transgression of the flow of sequential discourse. This is necessary because it is the apparent self-sufficiency and internal coherence of discourse which is responsible for the illusion of its independence, and by interrupting the progress of a sentence or a line we free its components from the chain of a meaning into which they are combined and return them to the already constituted meaning that is their source. Thus, as Barthes writes in his most recent publication, we pass "from simple readability, characterized by a stringent irreversibility of actions...to a complex readability (precarious), subject to the forces of dispersion and to the reversibility of symbolic elements which destroy both time and logic."[3] The result is a literature of multiple signifiers, in which, as Barthes explains in *Writing Degree Zero,* "the spontaneously functional nature of language" is destroyed and "only its lexical basis" is left standing.

The Word shines forth above a line of relationships emptied of their content; grammar is bereft of its purpose, it becomes prosody and is no longer anything but an inflection which lasts only to present the Word. Connections are not properly speaking abolished, they are merely reserved areas, a parody of themselves, and this void is necessary for the density of the Word to rise out of a magic vacuum ... Thus under each Word in modern poetry there lies a sort of existential geology, in which is gathered the total content of the Name, instead of a chosen content . . . the consumer . . . encounters the Word frontally and receives it as an absolute quantity, accompanied by all its possible associations.[4]

I shall not comment on this remarkable passage, nor on its historical assumptions, except to point out that in its every appearance the word Word is capitalized (as it is in the French);

perhaps there is something in that "magic vacuum" after all. Let us see.

On the sixteenth of April in the year of our Lord sixteen hundred and twenty Lancelot Andrewes preached a sermon before the King's Majesty. It was Easter day and Andrewes took his text from the twentieth chapter of the gospel of John, verses 11–17:

> But Mary, stood by the Sepulcher weeping: and as she wept, she stooped, and looked into the Sepulcher,
>
> And saw two Angels, in white, sitting, the one at the head, the other at the feet, where the Body of JESUS had lyen.
>
> And they said to her, Woman, why weepest thou? Shee said to them, They have taken away my LORD, and I know not where they have laid Him.
>
> When she had thus said, she turned her selfe about, and saw JESUS standing, and knew not that it was JESUS.
>
> JESUS saith to her, Woman, why weepest thou? Whom seekest thou?
>
> Shee (supposing He had been the gardiner) said to Him, Sir, if thou have borne Him hence, tell me where thou hast laid Him, and I will take Him thence.
>
> JESUS saith to her, Mary. She turned herselfe, and said to Him, Rabboni; that is to say, Master.
>
> JESUS said to her, Touch Me not; for I am not yet ascended to My Father: But, goe to My brethren, and say to them, I ascend to my Father and to your Father, and to my GOD and your God.[5]

This text is appropriate not only to that day in 1620 but to our purposes here, for it is very obviously a narrative, answerable in every way to Aristotle's criteria for a well constructed plot, "a whole . . . which has beginning middle and end":

> A beginning is that which does not itself follow anything by causal necessity, but after which something else naturally is or comes to be. An end, on the contrary, is that which itself naturally follows some other thing, either by causal necessity or as a rule, but has nothing following it. A middle is that which follows something as some

other thing follows it. Plots that are well planned, therefore, are such as do not begin or end at haphazard, but conform to the types just described. (*Poetics* vii, 1450b)[6]

Aristotle's terms, as one commentator has observed, "connote not space and structure but time and causal movement, a sense of progress to completion."[7] The assertion is that in a good plot sequence, rather than chance or haphazard arrangement, is revelatory of meaning; that event follows event in a probable and inevitable manner; and that this is a condition not only of the action as it is formally describable, but of our *reception* of the action, whose full meaning is revealed to us even as the characters discover it, *in time*. What is discovered in the course of this action is Christ, who is first sought and then, as we might reasonably expect, found. There is however at least one sentence in the sermon which suggests something altogether different:

> He is found of them that seeke Him
> > not
> > but
> of them that seeke Him
> > never
> > but
> > found. (538)

What interests me in this sentence (as some of you will have guessed) is the number of adjustments required to negotiate it. No adjustment would be necessary at all were it to end as it might well have, at the first point of natural closure—"he is found of them that seeke him"—for this unit is both superficially and deeply satisfying: superficially satisfying because the stresses of sense and rhythm coincide ("He is *found* of them that *seeke* Him"), and deeply satisfying because in its unfolding the sequence is answerable to several of our expectations: (1) the expectation of empirical cause and effect (that is, you are more likely to find something if you look for it), (2) the expectation of finding this empirical causality reflected in the relational logic of discourse, and (3) the *moral* expectation that, if he is to be found by anyone, it should be by those who seek him, for as the scriptures tell us, "Seek and ye shall find." Every one of these expectations falls before the word "not," for we are forced by it not only to revise our understanding of the sequence, but to give up the assumptions which had made that understanding both probable and attractive.

As a result, we are for a moment without bearings, but only for a moment, since the very next word invites us to stabilize the sentence by predicting a new direction for it. As an adversative conjunction, "but" signals an antithesis and it helps us to domesticate the reversal of the relationship between seeking and finding by allowing us to anticipate its extension to those who *do* seek him. It is not ideas that make the mind uncomfortable, but the difficulty of managing them, and we adjust to the unexpected and unwanted complication of "not" by making it the basis of a new projection of the shape the sentence will finally take. That shape very quickly becomes the shape of a chiasmus, one of the most firmly directing of schematic figures, and with every succeeding word the reader is more securely (in two senses) locked into the pattern of the figure and therefore into the sense that pattern is encouraging him to make. Both sense and pattern hold through the word "never" where suddenly we are met with another complication in the form of a second "but." This "but" does not perform a clearly adversative function, nor can it be handled by simply reversing direction, for this only precipitates a clash between the two "buts," one so obligingly orienting, the other so egregiously *dis*orienting. The only option that remains then is to go forward, not in confidence, but in the hope of finding some help in what remains of the sentence. What we find is "found," the word we least expect precisely because it was so firmly expected after "never." Had it appeared then, "found" would have completed the contrast of the chiasmic

63

pattern—"He is found of them that seeke Him not, but of them that seeke Him *never* found"—but placed as it is after "but," "found" subverts that pattern and makes the sentence and its experience circular.

Some of you may want to object that my analysis of the sentence is more torturous and torturing than the reader's experience of it. And you would be right. For although the experience does, I think, involve the disruptions I have described, it is itself not disrupting but satisfying, and it is satisfying because in the end the sentence gives you exactly what you want and once had, the comfort of the assumptions which led you to welcome its opening words. That is to say, by leaving its discursive track and leaving you to stumble into its conclusion, the sentence returns you to the security of its first clause, but only after you have forsaken that security—o ye of little faith—for the problems raised by the syntax. What this means is that while you finally get what you want, it is not what you expect or when you expect it; you expect "found" to appear after "never," even though its appearance there, while locally satisfying, would be ultimately disconcerting (but those who seek him *should* find him); but you get "found" after "but" where it is locally disconcerting but ultimately satisfying. That is, while you find "found,'" you find it independently of the discursive operations you have been performing, and therefore it could be more truly said that *found finds you.*

This is exactly what happens in the sermon, not only to Mary Magdalene, but to Andrewes and his parishioners, all of whom spend a great deal of time looking for something that has already found them. What Andrewes is looking for are things that fit together, correspondences, agreements, and he begins by commenting with satisfaction on the appropriateness of the day to the text: "It is *Easter-day* abroad: And it is so in the Text. We keep *Salomons* rule (531)." The keeping of Solomon's rule ("on the day of the Word, so this day") is not only a point of honor for Andrewes, but a source of security, for by Solomon's rule at least the first step of his exegetical exercise can be validated. In another sermon it occurs to him that he is *not* keeping Solomon's rule—his text, he admits, comes "a little too soone, before the time and should have staied till the day it was spoken on rather than on this day"—and he is at pains to find a rationale for thus proceeding out of order. Like any other interpreter, then, Andrewes worries about his method of analysis and exposition, and in the early stages of the sermon he is very careful both to introduce the machinery of his exposition and to continually point out to us that it is processing the meaning he seeks:

To look a little into it. 1. *Mary* is the name of a woman: 2. *Mary Magdalene,* of a sinful woman.
That, to a woman first, it agreeth well, to make even with *Eve;* that as by a woman came the first newes of death; so by a woman also might come the first notice of the Resurrection from the dead. And the place fits well, for, in a garden, they came, both.
That to a sinful woman first; that also agrees well. To her first that most needed it, and so first sought it. And it agrees well, He be first found of her that first sought Him. (532)

What kind of agreements are these? First of all they are exclusive agreements, in the sense that for the phrase "it agrees well" one might substitute "it is fitting," and this in turn implies that were it otherwise, were Mary Magdalene neither sinful nor a woman, it would not be fitting. In the second place (for we are now exegetes of the exegesis) these are agreements which agree with our common sense of the way the world is and should be. Andrewes here sounds curiously like the Puritan preachers for whom he and Donne were the evil exemplars of a self-glorying virtuosity; the style is plain; what repetitions there are support the unfolding of the argument, the argument is easy to follow, and it is itself followed by an application or "use": "In which two, there is opened unto us *a gate of hope . . .*

one, that no infirmity of sex ... the other, that no enormity of sinne ... shall debarre any to have their part in CHRIST (532)." In short, one thing is succeeding another in a meaningful and meaning-producing order, and both Andrewes and his parishioners are finding what they want which is also what they expect. And then something very curious happens; the schemes or divisions which are to serve as a framework for the sermon proliferate; first there is the division of the three parties, Mary, the Angels, and Christ, each of whom is further divided into his or her parts; these divisions are followed immediately by a fourfold division of the favor vouchsafed unto Mary this day, and that in turn by a tenfold division of the love by which she merited that favor. One division is helpful, two are complicating, four are impossible, and as these succeed one another without interruption and without exposition, they operate to inhibit rather than facilitate the forward progress of the sermon; rather than providing direction for the listener (as the handbooks claim) they give him more directions than he can comfortably manage.

This change in the pace and mode of the sermon coincides with a change in its language, which is now more recognizably the language of Lancelot Andrewes:

We cannot commend her faith; her love, wee cannot but commend; and so doe: Commend it in her, commend it to you. Much it was, and much good proofe gave she of it. Before, to *him* living; now, to *Him* dead. To Him dead, there are diverse; 1. She was last at His crosse, and first at His grave; 2. Staied longest there, was soonest here; 3. Could not rest, till she were up to seeke Him; 4. Sought Him, while it was yet darke, before she had light to seeke Him by. (533)

There are in this passage two organizational forces, one represented by the sequence of numbers and the other *created* by the patterned repetition of words and phrases. While earlier these two were mutually reinforcing, they here compete for the attention of the reader or listener. Moreover, the competition is

66

short-lived, for it is not long before the order provided by the numbers becomes secondary to the multiple and non-linear orderings of the proliferating verbal patterns. These are too many to be listed here, and of course their listing would be a distortion of the geometric manner of their apprehension; but one can point at least to the more obvious patterns of alliteration and assonance: good, gave, living; good, proof, before; dead, Dead, divers; divers, Last, Cross, first; first, stayed, longest, soonest, rest, seek, sought; sought, til, while, light. Notice that these patterns are both discontinuous and overlapping and that their components are themselves involved in other patterns of schematic point and contrast (*i.e.,* "Before to *him* living, now to *Him* dead"). To a large extent, then, the listener is not following any one pattern, but allowing multiple and multiplying patterns to register. The only constant element in all of these is the pronoun Him which thus draws to itself all the separate significances of the structures in which it momentarily operates.

What happens in this passage can be described by returning to the language of Roland Barthes: "the word shines forth above a line of relationships emptied of their content; grammar is bereft of its purpose, it becomes prosody, and is no longer anything but an inflection which lasts only to present the Word." Or, in more formal but hardly less formidable terms (they are Roman Jakobson's): *"the principle of equivalence [is projected] from the axis of selection into the axis of combination."* That is to say, the axis on which semantic units are combined into a meaning that is available only at the end of a chain becomes instead a succession of equivalent spaces in which independent and *immediately* available meanings are free to interact with each other, unconstrained by the subordinating and distinguishing logic of syntax and discourse. Sequence is no longer causal but additive; it no longer processes a meaning but provides an area in which meanings separately constituted are displayed and equated. This comes about in one of two ways:

either the relational links which make discourse progressive and linear are simply omitted (as they are in much of Andrewes' extraordinarily compressed and elliptical prose), or they remain but cease to function because they are overwhelmed by the logic of equivalence:

And as she wept, she stooped, and looked in, ever and anon. That is, she did so *weepe,* as, she did *seeke* withall. *Weeping* without *seeking,* is but to small purpose. But, her *weeping* hindred not her *seeking,* Her sorrow dulled not her diligence. And, diligence is a character of love, comes from the same roote, *dilectio* and *diligentia* from *diligo,* both. *Amor diligentiam diligens.* (534)

We begin with the narrative situation and with the assertion of a clash between weeping and seeking; but of course even as the two are separated by the argument ("*weeping* without *seeking,* is but to small purpose") they are joined by the likeness of sound, and, as Andrewes continues, likeness *becomes* the argument, repeated and extended in the transformation of seeking into sorrow and sorrow into diligence and diligence into love. In short, the axis of combination, the syntagmatic axis, becomes the vehicle for enlarging the axis of selection, the paradigmatic axis, and, as the sermon proceeds, the paradigmatic axis is enlarged to include *everything;* that is, everything is transformed into a character of love.

Now if the paradigmatic axis, the storehouse of equivalent and interchangeable meanings, includes everything, choice is less crucial than it would be in a world of real differences, and arrangement and order (the Aristotelian bywords) become matters of indifference, not because we are indifferent to meaning, but because meaning is available independently of our structures which rather than generating it simply display it. Thus the correspondences which Andrewes seeks and we expect are found not at the end of his sentences or paragraphs or sections, but in the equivalencies already existing in the materials at his disposal; and while these sentences and paragraphs and sections

68

can not help but bring meaning to light, we do not feel that they are producing it. Fitting together is in the nature of things; agreement is a condition of the universe rather than the product of our procedures. It is not that you cannot find meaning, but that you cannot help but find it; indeed, it finds you or you stumble into it as we do in the sentences of this sermon long before they come to *their* point.

What I am suggesting is that in the universe of the sermon, a universe which includes the reader and the preacher as well as the characters, it is impossible to make a mistake, or to fail to find what you are seeking (he is found of them that seek him not, but of them that seek him, never but found), but this also means that it is impossible to be right; you can not seek successfully precisely because your success is always assured. And in this at least the sermon is not a gloss on the story of Mary Magdalene, but rather the story of Mary Magdelene is a gloss on the sermon, for she makes mistake after mistake and looks everywhere but in the proper place, and yet she finds what she is looking for even as she looks past it:

For *they* (but she knew not who) *had carryed Him* (she knew not whither) *laid Him* (she knew not where) there to doe to *Him* (she knew not what). (536)

At each point where the question is asked—by who, whither, where, what—it is answered in an exactly parallel position by *Him, Him, Him, Him.* Even in her verbal seeking—and seeking is what a question does—Mary is found by what she seeks. What she seeks of course is Christ, and at the most dramatic yet anticlimactic moment in the sermon, anticlimactic because it is so prolonged, she fails to recognize him. "And so, CHRIST she saw, but knew *Him* not. Not only not knew *Him,* but misknew *Him, tooke Him for the Gardiner* (538)." But even as this mistake is reported it is explained away, first because it is understandable—"it fitted well the time and place . . . The time, it was the Spring; the place, it was a Garden (that place is most in request at that time)"—and then because it is no mistake at all—"though she might seeme to erre in some sense, yet in some other she was in the right. For, in a sense, and in a good sense, CHRIST may well be said to be a *Gardiner,* and indeed is one. For our rule is, CHRIST, as he appeares, so *He* is, ever: No false semblant in *Him.* A *Gardiner* He is then." The sense in which she is right is the sense Christ makes possible, for since he made the world it is proper to find him—and only Him—in its *every* appearance. Nothing can be miscalled in his name, for everything bears the imprint of his signature, and is a character of love, as Andrewes proceeds to discover by looking a little into the word gardener: "The first, the fairest garden that ever was (Paradise) He was the *Gardiner,* it was of His planting. . . . So, a *Gardiner* in that sense. But not in that alone . . . Hee it is that gardens our soules . . . sowes and plants them with true roots and seeds of righteousnesse, waters them with the dew of His grace . . . besides all these, nay over and above, all these, this day (if ever) most properly He was a *Gardiner* . . . who made such an herbe grow out of the ground this day, as the like was never seene before, a dead body, to shoot forth alive out of the grave . . . I aske, was He so this day alone? No. . . For, He it is, that by vertue of this mornings act, shall garden our bodies, too: turne all our graves into garden-plots (538–9)." (Dare I hope for a pun?) This amazing sequence ends not merely by clearing Mary Magdalene of error but by implying that she would have been in error had she done otherwise: "So then: He appeared no other, than He was; a *Gardiner* Hee was, not in shew alone, but *opere et veritate,* and so came in His owne likenesse." Of course, this would have been the case no matter what or whom she had mistaken him for; the operation performed on this word could have been performed on any other. Christ's own likeness is everything in the world he has created and, just as his omnipresence makes it impossible not to find him, so is it impossible to say anything of him that is not true. One can even charge him, as Mary does, with being "a breaker up of graves, a carryer away of Corses." Her "if thou have borne him hence" as Andrewes observes, "implies as much." And yet he marvels, "see how GOD shall direct the tongue! In thus charging Him ... She sayes truer than she was aware. For indeed, if any *tooke Him away*, it was Hee did it. So, shee was not much amisse. Her *si tu*, was true, though not in her sense ... This was true, but this was no part of her meaning (540)."

Here we come to the crux of the matter, not only with respect to Mary and her seeking, but with respect to the expository machinery of the sermon; both succeed but through no fault of their own and both are overtaken by the meaning they seek, Mary when she looks past what she has already found, and the sermon when its sentences yield what they are seeking (and what we expect) before their linear course is run; her inability to say amiss is matched by the inability of the language to refrain from displaying correspondences; both succeed accidentally in the sense that they have access to what they find not because they elucidate it, but because they are a part of it and involuntarily trace out what *it* has inscribed in *them;* they do not find a meaning, but live in it and so declare it in everything they do.

For Mary Magdalene, for Andrewes, and for us the moral is the same: if the paradigmatic axis, the storehouse of already constituted and interchangeable meanings, includes everything, it also includes the structures by means of which we validate and assert our independence; we, no less than the words we speak, are meant, stipulated, uttered by another; in our postures as seekers, after meaning or after Christ (they are of course the same), we place ourselves outside a system and presume to make sense of it, to fit its parts together; what we find is that the parts are already together and *that we are one of them,* living in the meaning we seek—"in him we live and move and have our meaning"—not as its exegetes but as its bearers; we are already where we want to be and our attempts to get there —by writing, by reading, by speaking—can do nothing else but extend through time the "good news" of our predetermined success.

The sequence of our lives, then, in the life of the reading experience, is exactly like the sequence of this sermon; proceeding from point to point, but in a progression that is not generating meaning but merely creating new spaces into which the meaning that is already there expands; the syntagmatic axis, in all of its manifestations—in discourse, in history, in time itself—is simply a succession of areas in which the paradigmatic equivalences are made manifest. Every "but" is an "and," every "however" an "also," and every transition is nothing more than an opportunity to take a breath. In Aristotelian terms, *everything is middle,* even when there are, as there are in this sermon, all the formal signs of a beginning and an end.

In this sermon those signs suffer the fate reserved for all relational links in seventeenth-century anti-narrative; they become irrelevant. You will recall that in the opening paragraphs a great deal of emphasis is placed on the manner of the division or divisions, and it might have occurred to you, and it is certainly occurring to you now, that I have paid no attention to those divisions at all. This omission is precisely true to the experience of the sermon, for the life of that experience inheres in the proliferation and cross-indexing of innumerable and interrelated patterns, and that life flows independently of the numbers which regularly but irrelevantly interrupt and segment it. This is not an irrelevance we bother about, because we are aware of it only at two points. The first is immediately after Mary Magdalene has been praised for being right despite herself: "This was true, but this was no part of *her* meaning." Andrewes then pauses to say, "I can not here passe over two more

Characters of her love, that so you may have the full ten I prom-
ised (540)." This aside is gratuitous exactly in the measure that
we have long since ceased to expect the full ten or any other
number.

That is to say (and I have said it before), we have been getting what we want rather than what we expected, and what
we expected is no longer controlling or even remembered. The
organization of the sermon, the arrangement of its parts, is no
more responsible for the meanings that have been brought to
light than Mary is responsible for the meaning her words find.
Indeed, the relationship is even more oblique, for what she
finds at least validates her intention if not her perception, while
what the structure of the sermon finds is simply what is there
in any case. Ten is an arbitrary number signaling the end of an
arbitrary sequence; any number would have done, any order
would have served; it is a matter of indifference, an indifference
Andrewes displays openly when he closes or rather stops by
remarking: "I see, I shall not be able to goe further than this
verse (542)." Here we see exactly how time is at once everything and nothing; presumably the bell has rung and he must
give over, but while time has run out, the sermon is nevertheless
complete, for the meaning it offers is found not at the end of it,
in the *fullness* of time, but at every point in its temporal succession. Am I then arguing that the parts of the sermon could
be rearranged with no loss of coherence or power? Not at all,
for, paradoxically, it is the sequence of the sermon as it stands
that leads us to affirm the irrelevance of sequence. The experi-
ential point is realized only through the agency of the structure
it subverts, which becomes, in effect, the vehicle of its own
abandonment.

When I was asked to write this paper I worried a great deal
because it seemed to me that there weren't very many narratives
in the seventeenth century to be theoretical about, but of course
this has long since become my point. A good plot, Aristotle tells

73

us, is a series of irreversible actions leading to a conclusion that has been determined by the intersection of character and choice with circumstance, a chain of events each of which is significant by virtue of its relationship to a *developing* meaning. But a Christian plot, in the sense that there is one, is haphazard, random in its order, heedless of visible cause and effect, episodic, inconclusive, consisting of events that are both reversible and interchangeable. This is more, however, than an incompatibility of aesthetics; for the logic of narrative, of sequential causality, is the logic of human freedom and choice: the freedom to take a step that is determining and the choice to be a character in an action that is either fortunate or unfortunate. Within a Christian framework, however, the plot is fortunate by divine fiat, and one reaches a point not because he chooses, but because he has been chosen, that is, redeemed. The price we pay for this redemption is the illusion of self-sufficiency and independence, the illusion of moving toward a truth rather than moving by virtue of it and within it, the illusion that destiny and meaning are what we seek rather than what has sought, and found, us. It is finally, of course, a question of epistemology, and I return once more to Lancelot Andrewes: "The *Apostle* saith, *Now we have knowne* GOD, (and then correcteth himself) *or rather have been knowne of* GOD. For till He know us, we shall never know Him aright (541)."

This anatomy of knowing is exactly the opposite of what we naturally assume, and our natural assumptions are reflected in the flow of discursive and sequential thought which implicitly claims for itself, and therefore for us from whom it issues, the responsibility for making and elucidating meaning. If we are to disengage ourselves from these claims, they must not only be raised to the level of consciousness, but their supports in language must be made spectacularly non-functional. This is why in Andrewes' sermons, and in the other great monuments of seventeenth-century prose, temporal structures—the signs of connection and relation—are not omitted but exaggerated, emptied of their explanatory and organizing powers, but remaining nevertheless as "merely reserved areas, a parody of themselves."[9] The bad faith of referential language is removed by making the forms of that language—logic, subordination, definition, sequence—conspicuously irrelevant to the meaning which overwhelms them, a meaning of which they are not independent, although it is independent of them, a meaning which is found no matter where or how or with what indifferent means it is sought, for, he is found of them that seek him not, but of them that seek him never but found.

Notes

1. Paul Ricoeur, "Symbole et temporalite," in *Archivo di Filosofia,* no. 1–2 (Rome, 1963), p. 24.

2. Roland Barthes, "Science Versus Literature," in *Structuralism: A Reader,* ed. Michael Lane (London: Cape, 1970), p. 414.

3. Roland Barthes, "Action Sequences," in *Patterns of Literary Style,* ed. Joseph Strelka (University Park, Pa.: Pennsylvania State University Press, 1971), p. 14.

4. Roland Barthes, *Writing Degree Zero,* trans. Annette Lavers and Colin Smith (London: Cape, 1967), pp. 52–54.

5. Lancelot Andrewes, *XCVI Sermons,* 3rd edition (London: printed by Richard Badger, 1635), p. 531.

6. The translation is C. S. Baldwin's, taken from his *Ancient Rhetoric and Poetic* (Gloucester, Mass.: Smith, 1959), pp. 148–49.

7. Baldwin, *Ancient Rhetoric and Poetic,* p. 149.

8. "Linguistics and Poetics," in *Style in Language,* ed. T. Sebeok (Cambridge, Mass.: M.I.T. Press, 1960), p. 358.

9. For a demonstration and expansion of this thesis, see my *Self-Consuming Artifacts: The Experience of Seventeenth Century Literature* (Berkeley and Los Angeles: University of California Press, 1972).

IV

Theory of the ΛΟΓΟΙ
The Speeches in Classical and
Renaissance Narrative

RICHARD A. LANHAM

Aᴛ ᴏɴᴇ ᴘᴏɪɴᴛ in *Northanger Abbey,* Miss Tilney asks Catherine Morland, that voracious consumer of Gothic Romance, if she likes to read history. She does not.

"I read it a little as a duty," she says, "but it tells me nothing that does not either vex or weary me. The quarrels of popes and kings, with wars and pestilences, in every page; the men all so good for nothing and hardly any women at all—it is very tiresome: and yet I often think it odd that it should be so dull, for a great deal of it must be invention. The speeches that are put into the heroes' mouths, their thoughts and designs—the chief of all this must be invention, and invention is what delights me in other books."[1]

She spoke with a resonant voice. The speeches had not delighted anyone for a hundred years when Jane Austen wrote, and they have not gained in popularity since.

Speeches are everywhere in classical narrative, of course, not just in Herodotus and Thucydides, Livy, Tacitus, or Sallust. Almost half the *Iliad* and two-thirds of the *Odyssey* are taken up with formal speechifying. Lovers orate at the drop of a sigh in Hellenistic romance, and this practice continues unchanged up to Sidney's *Arcadia.* Orations were familiar school exercises for nearly 2000 years in Western Europe. They dominated Elizabethan drama as they did Athenian. They supplied the focus for theories of language, the example for definitions of eloquence, the public occasions for political discourse. Yet today we can't stand them.

As Ernst Curtius says, "Rhetoric impresses the modern man as a grotesque bogey." When the speeches purport to be history, we find them inaccurate, grandiloquent, superficial, "neither willing nor able," as Auerbach says, "to deal with [life's] breadths and depths." In fictional narrative, they delay the story, break the fictional surface, bore the reader, and in general abrade the Jamesian theorist in all of us. When they stand alone, as in Gorgias or Cicero, they seem worst of all—self-conscious and overdressed, tarted up with tropes and schemes that obscure the subject and expose the speaker's insincerity, his vulgar desire to impress. Thus in the case of Gorgias, E. R. Dodds sees a "dazzling insincerity," and J. P. Denniston tells us that Gorgias was able to develop his stylistic tricks so smoothly because he started "with the initial advantage of having nothing to say." Behind all these dissatisfactions stands a single objection: not to the decorous high style but to the ornate style, the self-conscious style, the style that shows and shows off. From Aristotle to Northrop Frye the objection is the same. We might differ from Aristotle or Puttenham as to where the mannerism begins, but *ne quid nimis* has always stood as gospel.

An admirer of the λόγοι, then, must defend a narrative form —the alternation of story and speech—and the self-consciously ornate style that goes with it. And he must acknowledge that the object of his affection seems to most people an unnatural combination of Sir Fopling Flutter and Sir Tunbelly Clumsy, insincere, shallow, excessive, obvious, unreal, self-conscious, and without a subject. Modern apologies offer such an admirer little help. They amount, in a vulgar paraphrase, to "Well, they just liked that kind of stuff and we don't. And besides, don't forget, it enriched the language." I've often thought that rhetoric's only sensible defender was the great sophist Polemon. When he was dying, as Philostratus tells the story, he commanded that he be carried to his tomb still quick. As the sarcophagus lid was being lowered into place he was heard to exclaim, amidst the family's lamentations, "Give me back a body and I will declaim again!"

But things have not gone the way of this exuberant delight in words. In the ancient quarrel between philosophy and rhetoric, the West has increasingly sided with philosophy. We no longer enjoy, like the hero of an Elizabethan romance, "rolling in our rhetoric like a flea in a blanket." The reasons are not far to seek. Prisoners of an objectivist, scientific theory of knowledge, we stand subject to that yet greater emperor, realistic prose fiction. Both urge us to get down to facts, get on with the story, and to do so in a prose of maximum transparency. So long as we dwell in such an empire we shall, like Auerbach in *Mimesis,* never forgive rhetorical narrative for its failure to begin the realistic novel.

Narrative structure and verbal style are concomitant variables and both depend finally on a theory of knowledge. Only something so fundamental *as* a theory of knowledge, a way of seeing, could have impelled us to write off such a large part of Western narrative, could have led us to think its most language-conscious strand the most naive. As long as our conception of knowledge remains objectivist, scientific, truly in touch with the phenomena, the λόγοι and the narrative strategies they represent will continue to languish. We must become nominalists before they cast a longer shadow. In the ancient quarrel, we must incline again toward rhetoric, the symbolic, verbal way of knowing. To understand the rhetorical style aright we need, then, not a new theory of fiction, but a new theory of reality. Fortunately or not, we seem to be getting one.

This new theory of knowledge is only now seeping down to the literary critic. It stems, obviously, from the changed status of the scientific proposition effected by nuclear physics. The realization that a scientific proposition makes true statements not about reality but about the symbolic universe in which it chooses to conduct its discourse, brings with it a severe dislocation in human belief. The new emphasis on system rather than monad, on process rather than object, knower instead of known, affects us from the most abstruse theorizing down to our daily greeting, now no longer "Hello" but "What's happening?" It has been discussed brilliantly by Michael Polanyi in *Personal Knowledge: Toward a Post-Critical Philosophy;* it has led to the symbolist philosophy of Cassirer and Langer, to Owen Barfield's neo-scholastic effort to "Save the Appearances," to C. S. Lewis' plea against *The Abolition of Man,* to Whorf on language as a closed system, and to a great deal more besides. What it has done for rhetorical narrative is to free it from the paralyzing assumption that the primary purpose of prose is to describe objects, the primary purpose of narrative a sequential plot, the primary purpose of history a fidelity to "what actually happened." These objectives *may* prevail but they *need* not. Rhetorical narrative is free to be itself. T. S. Eliot said, in a famous phrase, that a poem's "meaning" is like the piece of meat a burglar throws to a watchdog to keep him quiet. Well, the new nominalism now tells us there is no watchdog. This not only liberates Robbe-Grillet—it does a good deal for Gorgias and Ovid as well.

The change finds its major literary statement in the writings of Kenneth Burke. Ortega had *posed* the question in *The Rebellion of the Masses:*

> But since it is impossible to know reality directly (conocer directamente la plenitud de lo real), we have no alternative to constructing our own arbitrarily (construir arbitrariamente *una* realidad) to *suppose* that things are a certain way.[2]

Burke set himself the task of analyzing reality as a series of such suppositions, or frames of reference. He sought for the master frame, for the viewpoint in whose terms the others might be related. He found this in what he called the dramatic hub, a world not of one stage but of many: "the ultimate metaphor for discussing the universe and man's place in it must be the poetic or dramatic metaphor."[3] Such a master-metaphor not only made the whole rhetorical and critical vocabulary available for the analysis of society, it threw primary stress on rhetoric, rhetoric as the *means* of creating a frame of reference, and rhetoric as finally the *substance* of that frame. Comparative stylistics thus became at a stroke the central study, not simply for the critic but for the citizen. Style, from the periphery of attention, suddenly moved to the center. For, in a very real sense, if one accepts Burke's metaphor, style is all there is.

For the most part, we might note parenthetically, the world has begun to accept it. (The new world picture, the dramatic one, is going to be—what a surprise—as literary as the old.) The mathematicians have developed a quantitative analogue, game theory, and sociologists and philosophers have—following Huizinga—extended the philosophical implications of its closed-field thinking. The psychologists and analysts, Freud with the famous discussion of play in *Wit and Its Relation to the Unconscious,* Piaget's studies, today a book like Erikson's *Childhood and Society,* have charted the role of this kind of thinking—under the game/play rubric—as a technique of socialization. The implications for a new theory of identity, for man as actor, implicit so often in Burke, were made clear in Mead's *Mind, Self, and Society* (1934), and have been elaborated by Erving Goffman, Eric Berne (in a popular vein), and others.

By the Second World War, and certainly after, the redefinition of the *Theatrum Mundi* metaphor which Burke had set in motion was pretty nearly complete. Virginia Woolf could write in *Between the Acts,* "He said she meant we all act. Yes, but whose play? Ah! *that's* the question!" It was indeed. Plotinus had premised a false outer life, a play, and a backstage inner reality, and this antithesis lasted long. But when you ask "Whose play?" everything changes. The tableau becomes a process, we become both actors and audience at once. It was only a matter of time before the theater people rearranged dramaturgy to conform with the new metaphor, so that now we have happenings, participatory drama, and the theater of the absurd, which I take to be the dramatic equivalent of a framed Campbell's soup can. When foreground and background become *choices,* there is no other way to go.

But, since this system-thinking, this preoccupation with frame of reference, seems today to find its center in Structuralism, we might spell out in these terms a few of the implications, *for narrative,* of the self-conscious, dramatistic world view which the Structuralist critics have inherited. The two main targets of the literary Structuralist critique, the traditional notion of *mimesis* and the "bourgeois" novel it produced, would both seem to bear on our theme. Both aim to poison Eliot's watchdog. Instead of imitating the world, they aim to imitate *wisdom,* if indeed wisdom be, as Whitehead tells us, "the way in which knowledge is held." The structuralist aims to involve us in a process by which *we* make meaning, *we* write the novel. So Ricardou says, "the novel ceases to be the writing of a history in order to become the history of a writing." Writing becomes an allegory of the frame-thinking Burke encourages and thus, as Barthes says, the novel becomes criticism. Mimesis is an analogy of function, not of substance. Since we not only invent a frame but choose which one to invent, choice and invention are the only really serious subjects left. The novel's subject can only be the *process* of making sense and this by writing novels. The introverted thinking of the closed system can go no further. The process of designifying language (in the sense in which Barthes borrows it from Shklovsky) is both pursued and imitated. Or, as Burke said in *Counter-Statement* in 1931: "The

84

hypertrophy of the psychology of information is accompanied by the corresponding atrophy of the psychology of form."

The Structuralists seem to have come to a position very like Milton's, when he selected the Fall of Man as the subject for *Paradise Lost.* They have selected the second Fall, modern man's irreversible acceptance of self-consciousness about what he knows and how he knows it, and for Milton's same reason. What else is left? Once you accept the circularity of language as a closed system (and, as Polanyi nicely observes, the existence of a dictionary proves this—words defined only by words), once you *speak* a language and thus commit your thought and self to its formal limitations, there just isn't any place else to go. The new, social construction of reality which, for critics at least, Burke began with the dramatic master metaphor, has led to a revolutionary stylistic position, now set forth in all its structuralist dogmatism. Form without content, or rather form as content, styles as thought, self-consciousness rather than sincerity, surface rather than depth, conscious, deliberate unreality, the writer as *poseur.* You all will remember these from a few moments ago, not as creed of a fashionable *dernier cri,* but as precisely the catalogue of charges traditionally made against the λόγοι. Not altogether without reason did Barthes call the Sophists his only forbears.

What surprises in this development is less that the Structuralist critics ignore the scientific, critical, and sociological matrix of their thinking, than that theorists of narrative, and especially students of the novel, normally a pretty trendy bunch, should have taken so long to catch on. (I must interject as an aside that I really do find it astonishing that someone like Tódorov doesn't even *refer* to Burke. Burke had covered the same ground—and covered it better—in the Thirties.) We then face a new theory of reality and a new theory of fiction derivative from it, both of which offer precisely the kind of environment in which the λόγοι, the whole domain of rhetorical style, can be seen anew. What conclusions about the λόγο, and about the opaque style, are scholars likely to come up with, as they go about the laborious job of rewriting the history of Western narrative? Let me state the case as strongly as I can, and then qualify it a little.

The first thing to go, obviously, will be the whole concept of a style as excessive. Stylistic excess is no longer possible. In as much as a rhetorical style overshadows the subject, it will simply become the subject—as it always has. The document will simply change its strategy and the critic will have to change his. Thus Burke wonders,

> ... whether the "artificial" speech of John Lyly might perhaps be "truer" than the revelations of Dostoevsky. Certainly at its best, in its feeling for a statement which returns upon itself, which attempts the systole to a diastole, it *could* be much truer than Dostoevsky. And if it is not, it fails not through a mistake of Lyly's aesthetic, but because Lyly was a man poor in character, whereas Dostoevsky was rich and complex.[4]

All the apologies for Lyly's "infatuation with language," and all such apologies for every other Elizabethan writer, simply do not apply. If *Euphues* fails, it is because Lyly's identity was a dramatic failure. This is what the book is about: the effort of a desperately alienated marginal man to create himself through language. And if he makes himself into a *vile* antithesis, it is no fault of the method. Of course *Euphues* is about nothing. That measures the chaos of Lyly's world. Language was the only core offered him around which to integrate a personality, and Lyly needed such a core desperately. The compulsive repetition of his style shows just that. The torrent of proverbs creates a horrible allegory of bankrupt proverbial wisdom, depicts the frightening insecurity of a world whose only truths were those of style. It is hard to see, in retrospect, how any style could better figure forth a search for psychic balance than Lyly's. After the historians of Renaissance fiction have finished sniffing at *Euphues,* they usually move to Nashe's *Unfortunate Traveller,* for comparison. Here is Life! Colloquial Vigor! Realism! Auerbach would approve. What one actually finds is the same hollow subjectlessness, the same manic prose trying through first one style and then another to become a mantic one, to work wonders and create a self, only to create Jack Wilson, a horribly faithful personification of schizoid violence.

Lyly suffers damnation in the literary histories, of course, just as much because he is not "sincere." Perhaps we can now see this Victorian red herring for what it is—not a red herring at all. Where insincerity has been a serious charge, there we are likely to find real psychological depth, a probing down to where the self evaporates into a series of poses. Shakespeare's *Sonnets* offer the best Renaissance example, and Castiglione's *Courtier* the best discussion of this; but the great monument, if I may sprint ahead a bit, is *Tristram Shandy.* There we see the bedrock the Structuralists yearn for, the real questioning of —and hence establishment of, validation of—the frame. Nicely enough for our purposes here, it is also a book about, a game made up out of, the rhetorical narrative tradition. Sincerity, in our dramatistic world, as in rhetorical narrative, is the only insincerity. Scholes and Kellog, in *The Nature of Narrative,* observe that the more rhetorical the character, the shallower. I hope you can now see how precisely wrong that statement can be.

From excess and insincerity we move naturally to lying, to rhetorical narrative's fondness for reporting what *ought to have been said,* a kind of high-class *esprit d'escalier.* The first lesson here was taught by the students of Thucydides, who pointed out how he uses speeches to illustrate the public world, the domain of *professed purpose.* Look, for example, at Chapter 6 of Book I, wherein is described one of the sparring matches which preceded the Peloponnesian War. The Corinthians try to convince the Spartan Assembly that the Spartans *should,* the Athenian envoys that they *should not,* go to war with Athens. Both speeches are good, the Corinthian—in its vivid delineation of the Athenian spirit—especially so. One really wonders what the Spartans will decide. But the wonder is irrelevant. And so, we soon learn, are the speeches. The Spartans decide for the Corinthians "not so much," Thucydides tells us, "because they were influenced by the speeches as because they were afraid of the further growth of Athenian power."

The speeches, then, are purely for display, form only a counterpoint to the backstage reckonings of national interest. The speeches dramatize public conscience. Three city-states offer themselves and each other pious truisms about treaties, traditional obligations, gratitude for past service, all as a cloak for their inevitable pursuit of self-interest. Thucydides' story is not only what people do and why they *really* do it, but why they *think,* and why they *say,* they are doing it. Or rather, that *realistic* motive is a combination, an interaction, of professed and expedient purpose. The speeches *must* be flowery and devious if they are to imitate accurately this deeper mixed motive. Thucydides wants us to see that these three city-states were fooling not only each other but themselves. He wants to show us how easily we hide behind fine words. He wants to make a statement about *language* and its role in human motive, and hence in true history. Are we to say, because the tape recorder had not yet been invented, that he was falsifying the event? Wasn't he really proceeding from a more sophisticated conception of event than "objective" history has yet come to?

As example of this tendency of the λόγοι to make language their real subject, look at another well-roasted chestnut, the famous debate at the beginning of Book XIII of the *Metamorphoses,* the debate between Ajax and Ulysses over the armor of Achilles. We must first notice that the debate is already a τόπος, having been taken from its Homeric context and made into a school-exercise. Thus, Ovid's reader sees it first and foremost, as a famous rhetorical occasion. He is not likely, as is the modern reader, to wonder why the issue wasn't settled with a little more dispatch. The *speeches* are the point, not the armor. They are not, though, unrelated to Ovid's larger design. He is in the midst of the Troy story and—if I may boldly and baldly summarize—is concerned to show a change in the concept of the hero, as Troy moves West to found Rome. Ajax represents the old ideal, the *rudis et sine pectore miles;* Ulysses is the new ideal, shrewd, political, above all verbal. Thus the τόπος takes on mythic overtones and these work very much to Ovid's purpose at this point in the poem. It also brings forward all the arguments for and against the two conceptions of heroism. It constitutes, in fact, a philosophical digression in dramatic form. The ultimate lesson the debate teaches is not, however, that Ulysses deserves the armor more than Ajax—Ovid's sympathies, in fact, seem to lean toward Ajax—but that the best talker wins. The verdict is given almost laconically:

> Mota manus procerum est, et quid facundia posset,
> Re patuit; fortisque viri tulit arma disertus.

The band of chiefs was persuaded, and what eloquence might do, now stood revealed. The eloquent man bore the arms of the brave.

Ovid doesn't bother to tell us directly who won, because the real winner is not so much Ulysses as *Eloquence.* The hero is now the talker not the doer. Thus the rhetorical occasion turns in upon itself; the self-conscious style ends up not only using rhetoric but talking about it as well.

Any speech set off like this, either by narrative or stylistic discontinuity, tends to turn in on itself and become—or stimulate—a meditation on the limits of language. Thus historical narrative of the rhetorical sort contains a sort of built-in control over its own veracity, a perpetual reminder to itself of the boundary conditions of truth which language sets. The rhetorical interlude perpetually analyzes the kind of statement the narrative plot is allowed to make. It will not let us think we know more than we do. By the side of it, "objective" history seems often a trifle naive.

Context, then, is crucial. What seems a sublime, if superficial, interruption may be a profound comic corrective. Only a sense of context can show you how the best history builds into itself a dialogue between the two ways of knowing. It is a sense of context which tells us that the *Old Arcadia* is a comedy, that relates the serious fourth book of the *Courtier* to the comic first three, that sees clearly the profound rhetorical comedy that Chaucer created in the *Troilus,* that reads rightly the back and front stage comic heroism of Shakespeare's history plays.

But I want to carry this matter of historical accuracy one step further. My text here will be the most famous oration ever composed, Cicero's *First Oration against Catiline.* Which of us can forget "O Tempora! O Mores!" or all the guff that goes with it, all the hot air about that famous Ciceronian consulship praised, as Seneca said, *non sine causa sed sine fine.* Yet, as an historical document, what is its domain? It is a document, an event. It was delivered. But delivered by one acutely aware of his place in history, aware that he was *making* history. His artifice is sincerity itself, the desire to act the role he has earned. His real motive? To play Cicero and thus to establish Cicero's reality. Further, this role is to be played by a speech which defines the situation and places it in time—and thus is itself an act of historical analysis—and also one which imposes that definition on *patres conscripti,* so that Cicero can then be the Cicero Cicero wants to be remembered as having been. All this is *secundam litteram,* "what happened." No objective narrative can get even close to an accurate mimesis of it. The decorum of rhetoric, a well-known history of narrative tells us, is anti-historical and anti-mimetic. Here—and almost everywhere, as I think—such a statement is *precisely* wrong. We can see here too the weaknesses of a simple-minded front-stage/back-stage debunking. "Reality" must come from both stages taken in all their complex relationships. Division into objective event and fictional coloration simply makes no sense.

Cicero's immense self-consciousness prompts a response to the fourth main charge against the λόγοι—shallowness of characterization, black and white motive. As we try to understand that huge and exuberant Ciceronian egotism, we come again and again to a motive essentially neither selfish nor patriotic but simply dramatic. Isn't this the lesson rhetorical narrative as a whole teaches? Burke had a phrase for such a motive—"pure persuasion," the actor's attitude toward his audience, but he didn't think the problem through. In a dramatistic, rhetorical world view, isn't the dramatic motive—pure pleasure in impersonation—the groundwork of all "respectable" motives? Is not acting the means of *establishing* the self? Sterne certainly thought so. And doesn't his mentor, Hamlet, move us profoundly just because he sees this, because he penetrates to the essentially dramatic nature of human motive? If this is not the heart of his mystery, that he knows he would rather unpack his heart with words than pack up Claudius with a bare bodkin, then Eliot is right that the play lacks an objective correlative. Structuralist—perhaps we might just say contemporary—fiction seems preoccupied with motiveless malignity for just this reason—it sees motive as amoral, as wholly aesthetic. Rhetorical narrative does better. It offers an imitation of dynamic motive, of the flight into and out of the histrionic center. Compared to this critique of motive, the profundities of the psychological, or of the structuralist, novel seem a little, well, shallow. Each sees only half of the self. For realistic fiction, the self is assumed to be central, whole, as "real" as everything else. For the Structuralist, dramatic only. But neither will see the other half.

We touch here the center of our nominalist view of rhetoric, a new definition of persuasion. One thinks of it as a changing of the opponent's mind. This is hard to do. This is the philosopher's way. Far easier—and here the Sophists and Madison Avenue are one—to change his self, to redefine him so that he will do what you like spontaneously, by desire. You'll recognize hypnosis at the root here, but psychoanalysis does much the same thing. (R. D. Laing's analysis of schizophrenia as bad domestic drama is perhaps the clearest case of this.) We must supply another frame. We must cast him in another play. If the frame is serious, we shall offer a game, one suited to our purposes, or vice-versa. As an example, let me take what is generally agreed to be the most outrageous rhetorical chromo bequeathed to us by classical antiquity, Gorgias' oration over the Athenian dead.

For what was missing from these men of what ought to be present in men? And what was present of what ought not to be present? Could I say what I want, I would want (to say) what is necessary, escaping divine retribution and fleeing human envy.

For these men possessed divinely-inspired ἀρετή but human mortality; many times preferring the gentle equitable to the remorseless righteous (or letter of the law), and correctness of grounds (or argument) to strictness of law, judging this the most divine and most commonly shared usage, with respect to what is needed and when (or at the needful time), both to speak and to keep silent, both to act and to let pass; and two things training in particular of what it is necessary (to train), intellect and bodily strength, the former by deliberating, the latter by performing; attending upon the unjustly unfortunate, punishers of the unjustly fortunate, stubborn for the advantageous, good-tempered for the fitting, with sensibility of mind putting a stop to mindlessness (of bodily strength), violent against the violent, orderly toward the orderly, fearless against the fearless (or causing no fear in those who cause no fear), terrifying in terrifying situations.[5] (Trans. Carol D. Lanham)

H. J. Rose apologizes for the compulsive σχήματα by saying that, though stale to us, they were fresh to the Athenians. Well, they weren't after the second line. And, of course, they weren't at all. Gorgias they knew. Unless they were naive to silliness, what pleased them? How does Gorgias work upon them? *We* are mightily offended. In the face of death we fancy a lugubrious sincerity. Who wants to be sung to his rest by a flight of *homoioteleuta*? But Gorgias knew the guard of honor was for the living. And he could not pretend the dead were not dead. He did not have our sentimental options. How console us? He could not change the event. How change our way of looking at it? Well, we have to have the sentiments. But they change nothing. How truly persuade us to do the only thing one can do about the dead, to forget them? He sets out a game and invites us to play. Name the tropes as they go by. Catch an antithesis by the tail. The more contrived the language, the more allegorical the style becomes—the more it serves its purpose. The meaning is not *weakened* by the style but *reinforced*. For it is the style which metamorphoses the grief into pleasure, makes us forget grief in the tremendous pleasure of expressing it. Gorgias' subject becomes finally man's tremendous resources of verbal pleasure, his endless ability to metamorphose one emotion into another by means of the word. Thus what is imitated is the *process* by which man can interpose words between himself and death, make of death a pleasure, finally—his self transformed—enjoy it. Gorgias deliberately makes the ostensible contrast between style and subject as great as possible, just to show us what he is doing. He wants to show us a new version of ourselves, man *in the process of* accommodating himself to death. Are we to say that Gorgias constructs a less *real* mimesis of how the human personality comes to accept death? Gorgias illustrates this technique of rhetorical narrative most brilliantly, but if you find my explanation uphill work, look at Cicero's oration for Tullia, which works the same way. Or, yet more clearly, Sterne's parody of it in *Tristram Shandy*. There he not only constructs a similar scene, Bobby's death, but forces us to acknowledge what he is doing.

I have now touched on, if just barely, the main charges against the λόγοι: no content only form, no thought only style, self-consciousness rather than sincerity, shallowness, deliberate unreality. I hope I've begun to suggest, by confronting the major offenders, how rhetorical narrative works best, most fully, and most like itself, precisely when it is *most* guilty of these charges, and how, given a dramatistic reality, these vices often become virtues. Allow me to conclude with a vague disquietude which is also a qualification.

Rhetorical narrative has escaped the severe task of founding the *traditional* novel. Has it done so only to found the *nouveau roman?* For the Structuralist position simplifies the Western narrative tradition as much as the objectivist. Doesn't someone like Barthes, at least, in his pretty bleak solipsism, imitate the sentimentalism of his existential godparents? If before we wallowed in bourgeois complacency as to what was fact, now we must writhe in existential doubt. We are, we flatter ourselves, really facing reality, chilly though it may be. As ur-type of this *nouvelle vague* of self-pity, here is Martin Esslin on the *Theatre of the Absurd*:

When it is no longer possible to accept . . . revelations of divine purpose, life must be faced in its ultimate, stark reality. That is why, in the analysis of the dramatists of the Absurd, we have always seen man stripped of the accidental circumstances of social position or historical context, confronted with the basic choices, the basic situations of his existence: man faced with time and therefore waiting . . . waiting between birth and death.[*]

But this is mindless! Stripped of all that makes him human, is man made plain? This is the critics' sentimental nonsense about *Lear,* Lear's nonsense about himself. So stripped, man is simply not man. You strip him of all resource, and then—how original, tough-minded!—you find him without resource. What is left out, finally (and here Sartre and Barthes are as one), is what Gorgias made the center of his theory of persuasion,

94

ἡδονή, pleasure. More especially, pleasure in words, in form, our immense and wholly delightful resource of words, our store-house of contrived purpose. The Sophists did not search for a center, because they already had one. Contingent it might be, but surely no more so than the human selfhood it served. Sartre's *via negativa,* the systematic critical destruction of all human purpose, has reached, in Barthes' Structuralism, its senti-mental extreme. The continual fuss about an absolute center has created what we might in a liverish mood call "center-mentalism," a steely-sighted, unblinking self-pity which invites us to ignore the resources for contingent purpose, for formal pleasure, which we in fact possess. Only thus can we savor the sentimentality of feeling so alone, of feeling so brave.

Tragedy, Santayana pointed out long ago, is sentimental. Well, our rootlessness has now become elegiac, consciously exaggerating the disproportion between our situation and our selves. The rhetorical dramatistic world view teaches a different lesson, and so does rhetorical narrative. Man's resources are equal to his dilemma. If he is cast into a formless world, the pow-ers that allow him to see its formlessness are the powers that allow him to impose form on it. Polanyi here seems to me to present best the modern version of Gorgias' plea for formal pleasure as the fundamental connection between us and the phenomena.

The understatement that language is a set of convenient symbols used according to the conventional rules of a "language game" originates in the tradition of nominalism, which teaches that general terms are merely names designating certain collections of objects . . . My own view admits this controlling principle by accrediting the speaker's sense of fitness for judging that his words express the reality he seeks to express.[7]

This accrediting of a sense of fitness, or "fiduciary commitment," which is what Gorgias finally means by ἡδονή, Western narra-tive allegorizes through objectivist narrative, through denotative

95

prose and the realistic imitation, through a narrative method which assumes that we can touch reality. By alternating it with a consciously rhetorical style, it suggests, in ways as various as its monuments, that both theories of knowledge are part of man's knowing, and have been so from the beginning.

We must realize that the rhetorical, Structuralist, like the objectivist, view contains forever within itself the seeds of its own destruction. The only solution is a literary form which allows us to alternate from one to the other, to live comfortably with each as it implies the other, to hold them both together as a single process. Thus the λόγοι, if they lead us into a solipsistic world of language as closed system, of motive as wholly dramatic, also lead us out again, lead us back to the phenomena, to an objectivist optimism that knower and known really have something in common. Rhetorical excess thus defends realistic narrative, in a surprising way *verifies* it. You must grant rhetorical excess its own aesthetic, that is, before you can see that it *is* an excess.

This symbiosis of rhetorical and realistic narrative carries with it an engaging implication. We shall have to describe more fully the ambivalent territory that stands opposite number to scientific reality, the reality that literary realism depends on. We shall have to devise another poetic, based not on the separation of literature and life—Frye's ideal order of words—but on two coincident spectra, one of style and running from least to most self-conscious, and one of reality, running from life to art. For the implications of rhetorical narrative and the dramatistic metaphor are clear. Literature is constructed in the same way that we construct reality. Objective narrative and fictional narrative, history and novels, differ in degree and not in kind. The difference, I would suggest if I had time, is one of scale, of magnitude and duration of being.

We must then rewrite the history of Western narrative as precisely the symbiotic relationship of these two theories of knowledge, ways to construct reality—rewrite it as the quarrel between the central and the social self, between society as drama (comic drama, one hopes) and society as highly serious, one-time sublimity. We must, that is, rehearse once again the quarrel between philosophy and rhetoric. And this time around, we must not simply use philosophy to debunk rhetoric, as the scientific world view has done. This is to make of scientific realism a system of idols. We must indeed restore the framing hypotheses, the "appearances," to the imagination of man. As Barfield has written:

The soul is in a manner all things, and the idols we create are built into the souls of our children; who learn more and more to think of themselves as objects among objects; who grow hollower and hollower. In the long run we shall not be able to save souls without saving the appearances, and it is an error fraught with the most terrible consequences to imagine that we shall.[8]

The most terrible consequences are the thinnings of reality's texture, the feelings of non-existence so familiar to us now as science's last best gift to a grateful mankind. But the most terrible consequences threaten also in the opposite procedure, the language-centered game-debunking of philosophy, of any certain connection between man and the phenomena. I have said that seeing Western narrative aright depends on controlling these two contradictory theories of knowledge. But surely as critics and teachers of literature, we must invert this. Upon seeing Western narrative aright depends our ability to hold together the two different ways of knowing which *together* makes us human. One is tempted to think this task new, but it is the oldest. Aristophanes, in the *Symposium,* at the end of his divided-self myth (a rhetorical myth, we might note, in a rhetorical context), poses just this task as the goal of love. And surely it is the goal of narrative as well: καὶ ἐπιχειρῶν ποιῆσαι ἓν ἐκ δυοῖν καὶ ἰάσασθαι τὴν φύσιν τὴν ἀνθρωπίνην, "and trying from two to make one, and to *heal* the human nature."

Notes

1. *The Novels of Jane Austen,* ed. R. W. Chapman, 3rd ed. rev. (London: Oxford University Press, 1965), Vol. V, p. 108.

2. José Ortega y Gasset, *La Rebelión de las Masas* (Madrid: Revista de Occidente, 1968), p. 196.

3. *Permanence and Change,* intro. Hugh D. Duncan, 2nd ed. rev. (Indianapolis: Bobbs-Merrill, 1968), p. 263.

4. *Counter-Statement,* 2nd ed. (Los Altos, Calif.: Hermes Publications, 1953), p. 43.

5. The Greek text can be found in Herman Diels, ed., *Fragmente der Vorsokratiker,* Vol. II (8th ed., ed. Walther Kranz [Berlin: Weidmann, 1956]).

6. Garden City, N.Y.: Anchor Books, 1969, p. 352.

7. *Personal Knowledge: Towards a Post-Critical Philosophy,* rev. ed. (New York: Harper Torchbook, 1964), p. 113.

8. *Saving the Appearances* (London: Faber, 1957), p. 161.

William Andrews Clark Memorial Library Seminar Papers

Editing Donne and Pope. 1952.
  Problems in the Editing of Donne's Sermons, by George R. Potter.
  Editorial Problems in Eighteenth-Century Poetry, by John Butt.
Music and Literature in England in the Seventeenth and Eighteenth Centuries. 1953.
  *Poetry and Music in the Seventeenth Century, by James E. Phillips.
  *Some Aspects of Music and Literature in the Eighteenth Century, by Bertrand H. Bronson.
Restoration and Augustan Prose. 1956.
  *Restoration Prose, by James R. Sutherland.
  *The Ironic Tradition in Augustan Prose from Swift to Johnson, by Ian Watt.
Anglo-American Cultural Relations in the Seventeenth and Eighteenth Centuries. 1958.
  *The Puritans in Old and New England, by Leon Howard.
  William Byrd: Citizen of the Enlightenment, by Louis B. Wright.
The Beginnings of Autobiography in England, by James M. Osborn. 1959.
Scientific Literature in Sixtenth and Seventeenth Century England. 1961.
  English Medical Literature in the Sixteenth Century, by C. D. O'Malley.
  English Scientific Literature in the Seventeenth Century, by Rupert Hall.
Francis Bacon's Intellectual Milieu. A Paper delivered by Virgil K. Whitaker at a meeting at the Clark Library, 18 November 1961, celebrating the 400th anniversary of Bacon's birth.
Methods of Textual Editing, by Vinton A. Dearing. 1962.
The Dolphin in History. 1963.
  The History of the Dolphin, by Ashley Montagu.
  Modern Whales, Dolphins, and Porpoises, as Challenges to Our Intelligence, by John C. Lilly.
Thomas Willis as a Physician, by Kenneth Dewhurst. 1964.

99

History of Botany. 1965.

    Herbals, Their History and Significance, by George H. M. Lawrence.

    A Plant Pathogen Views History, by Kenneth F. Baker.

Neo-Latin Poetry of the Sixteenth and Seventeenth Centuries. 1965.

    Daniel Rogers: A Neo-Latin Link between the Pléiade and Sidney's 'Areopagus,' by James E. Phillips.

    *Milton as a Latin Poet, by Don Cameron Allen.

Milton and Clarendon: Papers on Seventeenth-Century English Historiography. 1965.

    Milton as Historian, by French R. Fogle.

    Clarendon and the Practice of History, by H. R. Trevor-Roper.

Some Aspects of Seventeenth Century English Printing with Special Reference to Joseph Moxon, by Carey S. Bliss. 1965.

Homage to Yeats, 1865–1965. 1966.

    Yeats and the Abbey Theatre, by Walter Starkie.

    Women in Yeats's Poetry, by A. Norman Jeffares.

Alchemy and Chemistry in the Seventeenth Century. 1966.

    Renaissance Chemistry and the Work of Robert Fludd, by Allen G. Debus.

    Some Nonexistent Chemists of the Seventeenth Century, by Robert P. Multhauf.

The Uses of Irony. 1966.

    *Daniel Defoe, by Maxmillian E. Novak.

    *Jonathan Swift, by Herbert J. Davis.

Bibliography. 1966.

    Bibliography and Restoration Drama, by Fredson Bowers.

    In Pursuit of American Fiction, by Lyle H. Wright.

Words to Music. 1967.

    English Song and the Challenge of Italian Monody, by Vincent Duckles.

    Sound and Sense in Purcell's 'Single Songs,' by Franklin B. Zimmerman.

John Dryden. 1967.

    *Challenges to Dryden's Biographer, by Charles E. Ward.

    *Challenges to Dryden's Editor, by H. T. Swedenberg.

Atoms, Blacksmiths, and Crystals. 1967.

    The Texture of Matter as Viewed by Artisan, Philosopher, and Scientist in the Seventeenth and Eighteenth Centuries, by Cyril Stanley Smith.

Snowflakes and the Constitution of Crystalline Matter, by John G. Burke.

Laplace as a Newtonian Scientist, by Roger Hahn.   1967.

Modern Fine Printing.   1968.

The Private Press: Its Essence and Recrudescence, by H. Richard Archer.

Tradition and Southern California Printers, by Ward Ritchie.

Medical Investigation in Seventeenth Century England.   1968.

Embryological Thought in Seventeenth Century England, by Charles W. Bodemer.

Robert Boyle as an Amateur Physician, by Lester S. King.

The Life and Works of Eric Gill.   1968.

Reminiscences, by Cecil Gill.

Eric Gill, Typographer, by Beatrice Warde.

Mr. Gill, by David Kindersley.

The Flow of Books and Manuscripts.   1969.

The Case of the "Caxton" Manuscript of Ovid: Reflections on the Legislation Controlling the Export of Works of Art from Great Britain, by A. N. L. Munby.

Every Silver Lining Has a Cloud: The Shaping of the Newberry's Collection, by Lawrence W. Towner.

Some Aspects of Seventeenth-Century Medicine & Science.   1969.

Van Helmont, Boyle, and the Alkahest, by Ladislao Reti.

The Medical Interests of Christopher Wren, by William C. Gibson.

The Terraqueous Globe: The History of Geography and Cartography.   1969.

Edmond Halley and Thematic Geo-Cartography, by Norman J. W. Thrower.

On Chateaubriand's Journey in 1806 from Paris to Jerusalem, by Clarence J. Glacken.

The Task of the Editor.   1969.

The Ideal of Textual Criticism, by James Thorpe.

The Practice of Textual Criticism, by Claude M. Simpson, Jr.

The Lady of Letters in the Eighteenth Century.   1969.

*Letters of Advice to Young Spinsters, by Irvin Ehrenpreis.

*Ladies of Letters in the Eighteenth Century, by Robert Halsband.

The Private Collector and the Support of Scholarship.   1969.

The Book Collector as Public Benefactor, by Louis B. Wright.

The Private Collector and the Literary Scholar, by Gordon N. Ray.

Hobbes and the Epic Tradition of Political Theory, by Sheldon S. Wolin. 1970.

Influences on California Printing. 1970.

The Book Club of California: Its Impress on Fine Printing, by James D. Hart.

The Primavera Press, by Ward Ritchie.

The Primavera Press: A Bibliography, by J. M. Edelstein.

Charles Dickens and George Cruikshank. 1971.

The Fiction of Realism: *Sketches by Boz, Oliver Twist,* and Cruikshank's Illustrations, by J. Hillis Miller.

George Cruikshank: Mirror of an Age, by David Borowitz.

Some Aspects of Eighteenth-Century England. 1971.

Reason and Unreason in the Eighteenth Century: The English Experience, by J. H. Plumb.

A Walk through London with John Gay and A Run with Daniel Defoe, by Vinton A. Dearing.

Congreve Consider'd. 1971.

The "Just Decrees of Heav'n" and Congreve's *Mourning Bride,* by Aubrey Williams.

Love, Scandal, and the Moral Milieu of Congreve's Comedies, by Maxmillian E. Novak.

Theology in Sixteenth- and Seventeenth-Century England. 1971.

Fast Days and Civil Religion, by Winthrop S. Hudson.

A. D. 1689: The End of the Clerical World, by Leonard J. Trinterud.

English and Continental Views of the Ottoman Empire 1500–1800. 1971.

The Double Veil: Travelers' Views of the Ottoman Empire, Sixteenth through Eightenth Centuries, by Ezel Kural Shaw.

Sir Paul Rycaut, A Seventeenth-Century Observer of the Ottoman State: Notes for a Study, by C. J. Heywood.

Checklist of Turcica in the Clark Library, compiled by William E. Conway.

Changing Taste in Eightenth-Century Art and Literature. 1972.

The Art of Piranesi: Looking Backward into the Future, by Robert E. Moore.

"Such, Such Were the Joys": The Boyhood of the Man of Feeling, by Jean H. Hagstrum.

French and English Drama of the Seventeenth Century. 1972.

Tears of Magnanimity in Otway and Racine, by Eugene M. Waith.

From Corneille to Molière: The Metaphor of Value, by Judd D. Hubert.

English Satire. 1972.

Martin Marprelate: His Identity and His Satire, by Leland H. Carlson.

Satire, and Poetry, and Pope, by Ronald Paulson.

The Editor as Critic and The Critic as Editor. 1973.

Critical Problems in Editing George Herbert's *The Temple,* by J. Max Patrick.

A Critic's Apology for Editing Dryden's *The History of the League,* by Alan Roper.

* These seminar papers have been collected in a volume edited by Earl Miner and published with the title: *Stuart and Georgian Moments: Clark Library Seminar Papers on Seventeenth and Eighteenth Century Literature* (University of California Press: $7.95).

The Press has also published *England in the Restoration and Early Eighteenth Century: Essays on Culture and Society* edited by H. T. Swedenberg, Jr. ($10.00). A collection of essays originally presented, outside the seminar series, at the Clark Library, this volume concentrates on the period 1660–1800 in England. It contains contributions by Robert M. Adams, Bertrand H. Bronson, Jean H. Hagstrum, James W. Johnson, John Loftis, Maximillian E. Novak, the late C. D. O'Malley, James M. Osborn, and Robert R. Wark.

Both volumes may be ordered from the Press or from your bookseller.